Praise for *In the*

"Whether about coots, tawny frogmouths, wood ducks, or screech owls, Knapp's reflections manage to evoke wonder."

— *BOOKLIST*

"Pairing astute observations of birds and birdwatchers with philosophical musings about wilderness and identity, *In the Crosswinds* is a delightful, thought-provoking nature book."

—*FOREWORD REVIEWS*

"*In the Crosswinds* is a probing, bighearted quest for belonging on a tumultuous planet. Knapp, an ecologist with a philosopher's soul, draws inspiration from our feathered brethren to illuminate essential conservation truths. In a common loon or wood duck, it turns out, is the preservation of the world."

—BEN GOLDFARB, *Crossings*

"What can birds—wild and domesticated, migratory and resident— teach us about finding home in a restless age? Through exquisite attention to his avian mentors, Knapp gleans lessons for us all."

—MICHELLE NIJHUIS, *Beloved Beasts*

"With birds as his guideposts, Knapp reexamines the rich connective tissues linking life to landscape. Sometimes lyrical, sometimes wry, and always deeply thoughtful, *In the Crosswinds* is a journey well worth taking."

—THOR HANSON, *Close to Home*

"This book is an absolute delight, but there is a loftier take away as well: *In the Crosswinds* reminds us why we should traipse around wild places observing birds and the rest of creation. Such wanderings not only get us outside, they also take us outside of ourselves."

—ANNETTE MCGIVNEY, *Pure Land*,

"Knapp's witty and intriguing exploration of the avian world invites us to discover our own place amongst these fascinating beings and serves as a reminder of the natural world's enduring power to heal."

—TAMMAH WATTS, *Keep Looking Up*

"Fluid, fun and engaging; simultaneously thoughtful and thought provoking. An absolute delight."

—JAMES ALDRED, *Goshawk Summer*

"Knapp is a master educator, one who makes you ponder, question, and wonder. This book warrants multiple reads: once for the jaw-dropping beauty of his prose, and another to ingest the immense amount of information about our environment, especially the birds that are part of it, as well as where we as humans can find our places within. It's a love letter to our natural world."

—JENNIFER HILLEBRANDT, Townie Books

"Knapp shows how birds can deepen our connections with the places we inhabit. At once thoughtful and funny, *In the Crosswinds* is a joy to read."

—KATIE FALLON, *Vulture*

"I've yet to read anything by Knapp that doesn't rock my world. His perspectives on birds—and life on Earth in general—inform, provoke thought, and sometimes even make me giggle. Knapp knows so much about so much, and the rich, compelling stories he tells never fail to satisfy while still leaving me craving more."

—DAWN HEWITT, *Bird Watching For Dummies*

"Brimming with curiosity and a love for the world, Knapp's search for rootedness is both inspiring and full of winged joy. *In The Crosswinds*, birds appear as guides, tricksters, companions, and collaborators in a vividly evoked quest for grounded wisdom."

—DAVID GEORGE HASKELL, *The Forest Unseen*

IN THE
CROSSWINDS

IN THE CROSSWINDS

Birds, Humans, and the Paradox of Place

Eli J. Knapp

TORREY HOUSE PRESS

Salt Lake City • Torrey

First Torrey House Press Edition, June 2025
Copyright © 2025 by Eli J. Knapp

Published by Torrey House Press
Salt Lake City, Utah
www.torreyhouse.org

International Standard Book Number: 979-8-89092-005-8
E-book ISBN: 979-8-89092-006-5
Library of Congress Control Number: 2023952058

Cover art by Xavi Boa
Cover design by Will Neville-Rehbehn
Interior design by Gray Buck-Cockayne
Chapter illustrations by Linda M. Knapp
Distributed to the trade by Consortium Book Sales and Distribution

Torrey House Press offices in Salt Lake City sit on the homelands of Ute, Goshute, Shoshone, and Paiute nations. Offices in Torrey are on the homelands of Southern Paiute, Ute, and Navajo nations.

Table of Contents

Introduction

POORWILL

"Grab the strongest flashlight you have. Walk single file. And be quiet."

I instructed my thirteen ornithology students as the moon rose on the eastern horizon. We were looking for common poorwills near Tombstone, Arizona. Without strong flashlights, my students would never find the nocturnal, superbly camouflaged birds. Light illuminated the tapetum lucidum—the reflective layer—of a poorwill's eye and made it stand out. We walked single file to avoid stepping on rattlesnakes, a possibility I didn't relish explaining to parents who had entrusted their kids to me. The real danger, I felt, was for my students to return home without seeing a poorwill. Sleek, unique, and undeniably chic, poorwills were well worth the risk of rattlesnakes.

Rattlesnakes didn't prevent us from finding a poorwill; a six-ton whirlybird did. I should have known better. Earlier in the day, our rental vans had been stopped by border police. Now, a helicopter was off to our right, combing the ground with a massive searchlight. It seemed to be following a transect parallel us, a trajectory that might give us enough to time return to camp. A second encounter with border police, this one from the air, was another possibility I didn't relish explaining to parents.

"Let's look for poorwills some other night," I whisper-shouted to my crew. Abnormally quiet and apprehensive, nobody objected. Five minutes later, we were back in our campsite. Laughter replaced tension as the drone of the helicopter faded. We sat outside our tents reliving the encounter, high-fiving, and pouring sand out of boots. This random RV park had become the stage upon which we fled from border control. Our experience had transformed this simple space into *a place*, an interactive story we'd written in landscape and into our own lives.

A bird hadn't done it, but pursuit of one had. The act of following—pursuit itself—was worth pursuing.

The police checkpoints and the transect-flying helicopter were reminders that we weren't the only people moving along the Arizona-Mexico border. Like birds, humans follow opportunity. We migrate, some by choice, others by necessity. While I wanted to safeguard my students from awkward inquisition, I also wanted to expose them to complexity and to injustice in all its forms. To see that privilege is often a grand lottery, in this case dictated by the side of a line one was born on. Not all nests, not all places, are equally secure. Some are worth migrating toward, others better left behind. Lessons like this—as I have found throughout my professional life as a biologist, and as my students discovered that night—are woven into the search for birds. To learn their lessons, pursuit is required. And while I don't recommend leading a single file line of flashlight-wielding students into the darkness along the southern border, I do recommend pursuing birds wherever they lead.

The Hopi people refer to the common poorwill as hölchoko, "the sleeping one," for its uncanny ability to enter torpor. During this motionless state, the poorwill's temperature drops to 41 degrees Fahrenheit, its heart rate, from 130 bpm when active to just 10 bpm. Oxygen consumption drops more than 90 percent. When American biologist Edmund Jaeger found one in a crevice on a cold canyon wall, he was unable to detect a heartbeat or respiration. The poorwill can remain like this, as inert as a noble gas, for months. It can adjust accordingly when it's exceptionally hot. Among a colorful cast of travelers, the poorwill stands out for these bouts of stasis.

When conditions are right, however, the poorwill takes to the skies.

I sought a poorwill for my students, but I sought it more so for myself. I wanted to learn its secrets, to learn from an animal that lived and moved so differently. I wanted to find out what the bird could teach me about when to move and how to do so. I did eventually find one. In another year in another place with another group of students. That night, rattlesnakes were surely around, but choppers and search-lights were mercifully absent. That story isn't as interesting.

But the bird certainly was. It flew in spiraling arcs over a Texas madrone before coming back down to rest on a limb. The poorwill's outward orientation on the limb, with its tapering head-to-tail shape, melted it into the tree. It became invisible, a broken branch. Exqui-sitely and effortlessly, the poorwill melted into place.

We often describe a connection to place with a single metaphor: "roots." Particularly for those of us whose families were settlers, we tend to see our own search for place as a once-and-for-all kind of ques-tion. The poorwill showed me just how constrained I had allowed my imagination to become. Maybe, rather than obsessing over when and where we put down roots, we can lightly settle upon the land wherever we are. Close our eyes, exhale, and lean into the earth.

Birds are archetypal animals. (An animal is, technically speak-ing, any living being that can move.) To enhance their chances of sur-vival, courageous cohorts migrate, some spanning the globe, to take advantage of resources separated by space and time. I'm a member of Kingdom animalia too. Maybe that's why I felt so stuck. I reacted to these past few years of upheaval and uncertainty, as I tend to do, with introspection. But this time, instead of answers, I became more and more puzzled about my own place on this ever-changing planet. As a professor of human ecology, I literally study how people relate to the natural world. I no longer knew where I fit.

Having lost my own sense of place, I looked to the most accom-plished movers on Earth: birds.

Despite ceaseless travel, birds connect to particularity and to place. They are the grand masters of movement: They hop, run, flap, soar, stoop, hover, swim, dive, and even somersault. They heed invisible signs—the Earth's magnetic inclination and hereditary migratory instinct—to drop out of the sky, connect to landscapes, and refortify. Their connections run deep. Many birds return to the same nesting and wintering grounds. The golden-cheeked warbler, that migrates between Mexico and central Texas, goes one step further. Color-banded females reveal that the warbler not only returns to the same area but often builds a nest in the very same tree.

A bird's livelihood hinges on these decisions. The black-legged kittiwake chooses a sheer cliff for a nest, a place devoid of mammalian predators; if a suitable cliff cannot be found, it opts for an abandoned building or even a shipwreck. There, on a six-inch ledge or horizontal shard of rusted metal and with pitiless waves crashing below, the bird figures out how to live. To thrive even. Warblers and kittiwakes are not the exception, they are the rule. Birds travel, connecting to place wherever they go, wherever they are, and weather whatever changes come. I looked to birds—and followed them—to learn about connection. I watched other people watch birds too. And watched others watch me.

That's what this book is about: how pursuit can lead to being, and being to richness. Place, as I would come to discover, is a shared experience, something all creatures have in common, but experience differently. Birds offer us a winsome, unexpected invitation. By looking at them—to them—we can find meaning, absolution from feelings of isolation and displacement. I extend this invitation to you. Follow the birds as they flit among these pages. Follow them out into the world. Travel widely. Pursue wildly.

Wherever you go, settle lightly, melt into a landscape, and be. A desire to connect, and maybe a flashlight, is all that you need.

Peregrine

Having a tendency to wander

SWAN GOOSE

"White-fronted geese!" I jammed the brakes and pointed across Ezra's thirteen-year-old chest. Like periscopes, ten heads affixed to chunky bodies swiveled in our direction across snow-dusted corn stubble. I pulled over, handed my ever-present binoculars to Ezra, and conducted my well-honed drill: Take photos first, study the bird second. Birds are blessings, some arriving unexpectedly. But they can disappear quickly.

"You sure, Dad?"

"Hold on, this is better than that!"

"So these aren't White-fronted geese?"

"No, something's off about them..." I started zooming up on my camera's LCD screen. "One has a knobby thing on its bill."

"Actually two do," Ezra said, unable to conceal his joy in correcting me. "So what are they?"

"I have no idea. That makes these better than White-fronted geese."

"But I need white-fronted geese!"

"Trust me, you need these too." The need we referred to was acquisitive—aimed at improving our arbitrary life lists. Nothing about the word connoted dependency on the natural world. Regardless, a teenager needing a bird sounded better than needing a car, or more screen time.

"Rattle off the field marks, Ez."

"Top of the head: chocolate brown. Body: tannish-gray. Bill: dark, and then there's that knob that two have."

"Anything else?"

"Uh…not really. They're just round." Ezra loved tossing around whatever jargon he'd picked up, and he had no trouble abandoning it either.

"I'm gonna see how close they let me get," I said, easing out of the car.

"Dad, we're going to be late for the golf dome."

"Text the Millers and tell them we'll be late. This bird is legit!" The geese protested my approach with strident honking, each neck now fully extended with concern. Innate wariness was good; this implied wildness. If these exotic-looking creatures were wild, I'd just located birding's Holy Grail: a rare bird.

Well-balanced people don't keep score. Unbalanced birders do. Like hunters who hang racks of antlers in their living room, a rare bird is a birder's trophy. To arrive on scene to lay eyes on somebody else's rare bird is great; to find one yourself, to spend years sorting through similar sparrows only to, at long last, notice a different, out-of-place individual who belongs several states—or better yet, countries—away is the cup that giveth a birder life. Most of us don't have the patience, or skill, to find Waldo among the limitless lookalikes. But for the lucky, skillful few, they often post their rare bird online and savor the fallout of accolades. Two black-bellied whistling-ducks were recently found by an observant person—Robin—in Delaware Park in Buffalo. Rarely venturing further north than Alabama, "Robin's ducks" migrated faster through the cyber-nerd circles than they ever could have on their wings. Eager to join the paparazzi, I stepped out of a conveniently scheduled dermatology appointment, drove ten minutes through the city, and added to the fandom.

Robin's luck was now mine. By the time I climbed into bed, "Eli's geese" would be orbiting the internet, eyes would widen, jealousy would spike. Who would have thought that on this bleak, February day, Eli the indomitable birder would emerge? I took a few more steps. The flock galumphed through the stubble, honking louder. Heavy wings beat the frozen earth as each bird overcame gravity and launched away, barely clearing a hedgerow before disappearing into the gunmetal sky. A swirl of goose feathers billowed about in their wake, sprinkling the snow like confetti.

"We did it, Ez!" I said, rejoining him in the car and scrolling through my photos.

"Did what?"

"Found something awesome!"

"What are they?"

"That's the awesome part. I have no idea. These are so rare they're not in my field guide, at least not with the other geese." This was the one thing I knew definitively. Notwithstanding *Roll of Thunder, Hear My Cry*, which my fourth-grade teacher had coerced me to finish, my National Geographic *Field Guide to the Birds of North America* was the first book I'd read, memorized even. Except for one page, that is. An unworthy page entitled "exotic waterfowl" which wasn't worth my time.

"Good," Ezra said, "now step on it." Ezra might have inherited his sense of adventure from me, but I'm certainly not the source of his insistence on punctuality.

"Tell the Millers we found a rare bird. J.L. will understand."

"Already did while you were snapping pics."

My mountaintop of joy imploded a half mile down the road. A light blue house with peeling paint and a sprawling porch appeared. Skinny-wheeled tractors and rusty farm equipment pockmarked the yard; none seemed to have moved in half a century. Set back from the house was a period barn with a gaping maw, its doors long since being coopted for who-knows-what. Amid the loose hay scattered about the driveway was a goose. Black adorned the top of its head, ran down the back of its neck, and gave way to a grayish-tan body. A knob perched atop its black bill. I still didn't know what the bird was, but it certainly wasn't wild. Never have I hated the sight of a bird more.

Ezra, still texting the Millers, missed it. Rather than kill the moment, I kept quiet. Our itinerary was too good: an indoor driving range and time with good friends. If possible, we could squeeze in a peregrine falcon that somebody had found roosting under an eave of Foster Hall, on the University at Buffalo's South Campus. Golf shenanigans capped by a peregrine—too good for a stupid barnyard goose to squander.

Precious few golf balls went straight. They hooked and sliced, some remaining steadfast on the tee as our clubs whacked the turf or whiffed over the top. A few, to the chagrin of fellow golfers, managed backward flights. Wild trajectories were apropos. It mirrored my life of late. COVID was the chess master and I, as a recently tenured professor at a small university in New York, felt like a sacrificial pawn. While my university bravely forged ahead reinventing itself on the fly, I remained fixed to my square staring at bored faces in other little squares, that would disappear or go vacant like whack-a-mole. Anachronistic words from high school social studies lectures about the Black Plague became commonplace: outbreak, quarantine, isolation. New terms—facial shields, social distancing—added to the foreboding dizziness. If the virus didn't infect me, my inbox did, with its endless stream of nauseating notifications, mind-numbing protocols, and mandatory health surveys. An errant tick in the wrong box sent six more URGENT! messages into my inbox, each demanding instant response. Class attendance became pointless. Participation dropped to an all-time low. I couldn't blame my students. The experience was equally foreign to them. Often, the few brave students that did speak forgot to unmute themselves.

When Houghton returned to in-person classes, face masks concealed emotion and twenty-year-old psychology forbid speaking up. My syllabus followed attendance: disintegrating into a mess of crossed-out assignments and reconfigured due dates. My face masks reeked of yesterday's lunch, while my facial shield made me look like a low budget welder. Worse, it confirmed a fact I always denied: I was a spitter. Some days, logging in felt like the main accomplishment. Others, even that small feat was in jeopardy, notifications reminding me that my account would expire if I didn't update my password in three days. I wondered if I would expire first.

A quorum of shielded students sat before me, a dozen others zoomed in on a screen behind, and always—always—a technological glitch. Glazed eyes, pained expressions, boredom. Isolation. Teaching without connection. Life without joy. If my classroom was a roadside motel, Vacancy glowed ominously.

"Unheimlich," a German word connoting the commingling of the familiar and unfamiliar, expressed it best. I was unstable and ungrounded, feeling what author Robert Moor describes as "an experience of oneself as a foreign body." I longed for a mental and spiritual purge. I was asphyxiating.

In need of the Heimlich, I fixated on place. Place, whatever it was, seemed tangible. It offered mooring, sheltered ground to buffet the cold, isolating winds of academia, pandemics, and midlife. Psychological and spiritual stability seemed predicated on terra firma, a place to plant my feet and depend upon. Place didn't hit me ex nihilo. A tattered, innocuously titled book—*Land of the Seneca*—snatched from a yard sale, helped. The out-of-print book chronicles the lives of the Seneca, Indigenous keepers of the western door of the Iroquois nation, who inhabited the land well before my Euro-colonial ancestors did.

Arch Merrill, the author, didn't blow me away with his prose, but his catalog of historical place-names lodged in my head like totems. The places he detailed were the forests I hiked, the creeks I followed, and the present-day towns and villages I lived in and passed. While I had long used these names, I hadn't given their origin a second thought. Genesee, the river I kayaked with flotillas of students, translated "pleasant banks." Caneadea, the next town over, was "where the heavens rest upon the earth." Nearby Tonawanda meant "swift water," Cheektowaga, "place of the crabapple tree," and an adjacent county, Cattaraugus, meant "foul-smelling banks," in reference to oil that seeped up from the ground. Casconchiagon, "the place of many falls" became Rochester, likely because it proved too multisyllabic and ungainly for the colonizers' tongues.

Estranged and needy, I latched onto these sonorous, evocative words like smooth stones plucked from a riverbed. How many insipid names had unceremoniously replaced them? I lived in a small village named Fillmore, named after our forgettable thirteenth president, who, despite living much of his life in nearby Buffalo, never deigned to visit. Short drives anywhere took me through Cuba, Belfast, or Warsaw, foreign and meaningless.

Nothing is novel about this hackneyed mosaic of nomenclature. Many Indigenous names are lost. But some linger piecemeal, their meanings forsaken by our distracted, transient ways. The sad, shameful part is that I hadn't noticed before. It took an out-of-print book and a pandemic of schedule-clearing immobility to slow me down enough to notice. My epiphany was frightfully obvious: This place mattered to people long before me. It mattered differently, in a way I was missing out on. These words named places of meaning and nourishment. Land mattered. Rivers mattered. Trees mattered. Birds mattered.

Birds matter. This much I know. But can I know place through birds? Can I follow where they lead, migrate to faraway places and return? Do my frequent travels preclude me from fusion with the land? Can I connect with particularity as they do?

While the Seneca mercifully avoided Zoom calls and facial shields, heaven knows they faced other calamities, pandemics included. Crises the Seneca faced were of a different magnitude from mine. Who would have had time for time for midlife crises in the face of harsh winters, food shortages, and land displacement? Hitting midlife was a luxury, not a crisis.

Procuring a swan goose, which our mystery geese turned out to be, would have been a luxury, too. But the rotund bird wasn't here. Up until the last century, the swan goose, *Anser cygnoides*, lived only in its own native land—Mongolia and China. The flock Ezra and I saw on our way to the driving range was domesticated, a breed—either Chinese or African—brought over with the panoply of other domesticates now found in rural farmyards across America. The knob was a tip-off, as was its upright posture. Their wariness reflects a more recent domestication than say, the chicken. In the US, the swan goose is as mixed up as its compound name implies; it doesn't know what it is or where it belongs. I felt their confusion: Retreat to the barn or light out for the territory?

The swan goose did not grant me local birding celebrity status, but it did bring feralization into focus. In Latin, "fera" means "wild beast." It refers to any animal that throws off its domestic fetters to return to a wilder state, a metamorphosis I felt ready for myself. Domestication is a big deal, on par with advances in verbal communication, tool manufacture, and the conquest of fire. "It is true," Stefano Mancuso writes in *The Nation of Plants*, "that with the domestication of cereals humans resolved a large part of their food problems; approximately 70 percent of the calories consumed by all of humanity are produced by cereals. But in exchange, wheat, rice, and corn have obtained the chance to spread all over the planet thanks to the most important and efficient of all carriers: humans."

Mancuso makes it sound like a simple trade: calories for transport, symbiosis rather than subservience. Is it? What have I traded away for travel? Has my eager willingness to leave home left me homeless? Is my technological dependence symbiosis or subservience?

I love cereal, milk, and eggs on weekends. Plants, cows, and chickens don't seem to mind. We suppress their enemies, give them a warm barn, and fill their trough. Besides, if we weren't eating them, something else would. "Nevertheless the doctrine that all nature is at war is most true," Darwin wrote, "The struggle very often falls on the egg and seed, or on the seedling, larva, and young; but fall it must sometime in the life of each individual, or more commonly at intervals on successive generations and then with extreme severity."

At the root of domestication is influence, one group of organisms over another as a means to extract resources. Livestock cash in freedom for food and protection, like selling a house to enter a nursing home. I lumber out of the barnyard here for that's what I am: a swan goose, a confused transplant with a scrambled compass. Born into a place long inhabited by native swans and native geese. My history, hardly unique, is muddled by immigration and addled by a propensity to move; yet here I am, gathered up with similar swan geese. But I've grown wary of late—or maybe aware—that, much of the time, the simple business of life has distracted me from living.

In my rabble of weird birder friends, there are a few who deplore domesticated birds. They are the serious listers, whose greatest rush is a new tick on their all-consuming life list. (No judgment here, the struggle is real.) Birders covet unshackled wildness; we don't have time to waste time on dependent imposters who have gone soft.

A friend down the road recently texted me with news of a strange duck on his pond, hanging out with a gaggle of mallards. Not long later, the two of us stalked the perimeter Elmer Fudd-style. I filled a memory card with strange duck images. Like the swan goose, I didn't recognize it. Also like the swan goose, it exploded into the air once we'd crossed some invisible threshold of the duck's good sense. Torn, it circled the pond twice and disappeared over the tree line. Oddly, the mallards stayed put. Blasé, they preened as we walked away.

No high fives this time. I knew better. Unlike the swan goose, which was crammed onto a page in my field guide with ten other domestic waterfowl—this one didn't even merit inclusion. An internet search confirmed my hunch: This was a Pomeranian mallard, a domestic breed that had sprung loose. Its curly tail, white throat, and larger size were all telltale markings of a hybrid mallard. Who's to say why it took flight at our approach. When you're mixed up, it can be tough to know what company to keep. Or where home is.

I've begun to sympathize with these hybrids and domesticates.

I even search for them. It's not the Himalayan snowcock's fault that it now lives in the Ruby Mountains of Nevada. The monk parakeet, nanday parakeet, rose-ringed parakeets, and other transplants I've chanced into are also faultless. I share too much with these naturalized birds to begrudge them, governed as we are by thin attachments and mysterious urgings. Since I can't ignore them and can't count them, I compromise by penciling in a checkmark and date of first contact, a subtle nod to their adaptability and determination to persist. The graphite checkmark is intentional: These birds are significant but different, their attachments not as deep. Graphite or ink, it's a token of solidarity, acknowledgement that these transplants and I have peregrinated far from our ancestral roots.

The peregrine falcon certainly hasn't. Peregrines are found on six of the seven continents, native to all. Deft flying machines, they haven't needed a hand getting anywhere. While falconers prize them, peregrines hold domestication—and many of their handlers—in contempt. The one we sought had been reported roosting in an alcove of Foster Hall on Buffalo University's South Campus. As we circled the spacious campus, I couldn't shake the feeling that this was a fool's errand, worsened by my earlier swan goose gaffe. Foster Hall was as crenulated as a medieval castle. Thanks to the late hour, all the places a peregrine might roost were dark and shadowy.

"Sure you wanna try for this bird?"

"Might as well. We've come this far." Ezra's response didn't surprise me. While I had seen plenty of peregrines, he hadn't. He'd longed to see one ever since we finished reading about Sam Gribley's pet falcon "Frightful," in My Side of the Mountain. While rare sparrows haven't quickened Ezra pulse, peregrines have, thanks to their panache. They wing around like lightning, punch ducks out of the sky with balled-up talons, and are, judging from the growing number of pairs nesting in on skyscrapers across the US, incredibly adaptable.

Street lights flickered on as I put the car in park. Other than a lone police car inching along a circuit, the Sunday evening campus was deserted and cemetery quiet. "Judging from the photo the guy posted, the peregrine roost might be right there," I said, pointing to a white splattered sill.

"Could be from pigeons," Ezra said, unwilling to pass up an opportunity to offer a competing hypothesis.

"It could be from space aliens," I replied, scowling. "Shouldn't the bird be here by now? It's darker than sin." Ezra said nothing. I had struck out on many bird chases. He hadn't. Now he seemed to be grappling with the possibility. "Let's circle the building," I offered, "Maybe it has multiple roosting sites." I glanced at my watch. Home was an hour away. I had class to prep and papers to grade. Ezra had homework.

Hands in pockets to ward off the chill, we rounded the building in a wide arc, studying the ornate cornices below the roofline. Light from glowing computer screens emanated from a few windows; in others, heads bent over books. Binocular use would raise justified suspicion.

Back around to the front, I looked at Ez. He continued to stare at the roofline. Birding—the whole ridiculous activity—suddenly felt preposterous. Nobody in their right mind stalks around a residence hall on a midwinter night for the unlikely chance of glimpsing a bird. Foster Hall was surrounded by dozens of similar-looking buildings all boasting scads of possible crannies. Maybe this peregrine liked to mix it up. Maybe it was plucking the heart out of a pigeon twenty miles away in a park. Or cruising over Niagara Falls. Or enjoying the action in Atlantic City.

Birder hope dies hard. Ezra's chin remained defiantly up as he willed the bird to materialize on the building. I was torn. Would failure dampen his desire for falcons and future chases? "Okay, let's walk to that building over there," I said pointing. "If the falcon isn't here by the time we get back, we go home. This way we'll stay warm." Ezra nodded.

Off we trudged on the El Camino de Buffalo. Ten minutes later, skies devoid of movement, we were back. The whitewashed perch was still empty. "Well, Ez, I think…"

WHOOSH!

A feathered missile streaked overhead, banked hard, and swooped onto the sill in the exact spot the falcon finder had reported. In a world of infinite roosting sites, this peregrine had found one it liked. Fast, capable, adaptable—and loyal to a particular place. "Only the first inhabitants to occupy a piece of ground on Earth ever get to occupy space," wrote Dan Flores in his book, *American Serengeti*. The rest of us are just "engaging with someone else's previously created 'place.'"

The falcon kept its slate-gray back to us, blending in with Foster Hall's masonry. When it rotated around, its white throat gave way to an indecipherable mélange of thin, gray bars. Saffron eyes leered down at us.

We wordlessly passed the binoculars back and forth. While Ezra studied the bird, I studied Foster Hall. Why here? Granted this building had more personality than Walmart, but this place was so humble for such a majestic bird. Why this building, among so many taller, grander alternatives? Why this particular sill? What did this place offer which others lacked?

The peregrine gave Ezra more than a checkmark on his life list. It gave him an indelible memory at a singular moment in our journey together, a flesh and blood—and ridiculously awesome—point of attachment. It gave me a point of comparison. Swan goose versus peregrine. Round versus sleek, country versus city, domestic versus wild. Different, yet united.

Naturalization

*The admittance of a foreigner
to the citizenship of a country.*

There are some previously created places I don't belong. Mosh pits, red light districts, faculty meetings, and one I recently discovered: Royal Harbor in Naples, Florida. It was obvious the second I rolled up in my boxy, Chevy Impala rental car. The lofty royal palms were too perfect, the homes too expansive, and the cars outside the three-car garages too shiny and curvaceous. My net worth might have bought me one of the inflatable boats affixed to the luxury yachts in Royal Harbor's adjacent marina.

I was in search of a bird that didn't belong in Royal Harbor either: the rose-ringed parakeet. Though the species was well established, it hailed from Africa and the Indian subcontinent. The bird was innocent, a victim—or benefactor—of the exotic pet trade that has led so many species to put down roots in the palmy, balmy sunshine state. The parakeet had adapted quickly to Naples, just as it had in cities across Europe, Australia, and even Japan. While visiting my parents in nearby Fort Myers, I was having a harder time. Unrelenting stop lights, ceaseless strip malls, and my concern for Florida's wildlife in the face of habitat fragmentation and land conversion had metastasized into full-fledged anxiety. My sebaceous glands seemed to have metastasized too.

My arrival in Royal Harbor was more purposeful than the parakeet's. Two days before, Ezra and I had traveled up Florida's west coast to a place called "the celery fields," near Sarasota. We were looking for a greenish-blue, buffoonish rail with a blood red bill called a gray-headed swamphen. The swamphen, like the parakeet, had faraway roots. Before I'd shut the car door in the Audubon Center's small parking lot, a tight flock of aquiline birds arced past like a formation of the Blue Angels. They landed uproariously in the spindly tops of some small fruit trees bordering the lot. Wishing for earplugs, we stood slack-jawed as the voracious birds stripped berries off the foliage.

The fearless, neon-plumaged birds made the onlooking grackles look dull and obtuse. Winged extravagance writ large, the flock painted a sharp contrast with the earth-toned winter birds we'd left behind in western New York. A svelte jogger, sporting spandex extravagance, was equally impressed. Running in place beside us, he shielded the sun with a hand, awestruck. "Stunning!" he exclaimed, breathing heavily. "Do you know what they are?"

Rhapsody brought by the beautiful birds instantly dissipated. I hadn't the foggiest idea what these massive, radioactively green birds were, despite a lifetime of marinating in field guides, traveling around the world watching birds, and teaching ornithology. "Tell him, Dad" Ezra said. The jogger looked at me expectantly.

The temptation to make something up—turquoise-winged parrot, emerald parakeet—was strong. I could save face. The earnest jogger would be none-the-wiser, but here was my son. Pride? Or virtue? "I...I don't know!" I confessed, thrusting my hands in my pockets.

"No matter," the jogger replied, trotting off.

I disagreed. It mattered. The birds' beauty was arresting, but my nomenclature failure nullified it. Names matter. This was Florida, not the Amazon. There are a finite number of species. How had I never seen nor heard of this thermos-sized, incandescent bird? My trusty field guide to the birds of North America had included the exotic swan goose, I had simply failed to learn it. This flamboyant species, native to South America, had naturalized too recently to be included. When the Audubon Center opened, I hurried inside. "What are those gaudy big parrots out there?"

"Nanday parakeets," the volunteer replied. "Introduced. They've lived here in Sarasota almost three decades now."

"Never again, Ez," I said as we went off in search of a swamphen.

"Never again what?" He hadn't noticed the psychological turmoil spawned by my ignorance.

"Never again will I be surprised by a bird like this." Ezra shrugged, too well-balanced to comprehend how the world's fate hung upon my esoteric ineptitude.

To make amends, I'd made this solo pilgrimage to Royal Harbor. My failure to recognize the nanday parakeet was due to my overreliance on my cherished—but dated—childhood field guide. Like so many other birders, I had dismissed the growing army of avian immigrants as lesser beings and had blown off learning them. No longer. The world was changing. Birds, released by tired owners or canny escapees from aviaries, were naturalizing everywhere and adapting quickly to rapidly developing, tropical Florida. A quick Google search exposed the unexpected reality: swamphens and nanday parakeets were no longer an exotic exception, they were the norm. At last count, seventeen species had naturalized to Florida.

We don't think about naturalization very often, which is odd because many Americans like me have naturalized, or integrated, in recent memory. Birders' tacit bias against such species has a whiff of hypocrisy; we don't bother to learn them, are surprised to meet them, and judge their merits according to an arbitrary threshold of time they've spent in-country, making their worth whimsical and contingent.

With the Cornell Lab of Ornithology's eBird as my starting point, I decided to overcome my bias by tracking down and paying respects to the remaining sixteen transplants on the list. The closest happened to be rose-ringed parakeets hanging out in Royal Harbor. "Rose-ringed parakeets seen at a backyard feeder in a vacant lot across the canal on

Snook Drive," one phlegmatic birder reported on the site.

Shouldn't be hard to find, I reasoned. I had the community, the street, and a clue—the vacant lot. This was a far cry from my usual quests, many of which had me swatting mosquitos, dehydrated, or sun scorched. This ritzy enclave called for cool nonchalance rather than survival skills. It was a trait I coveted in high school. Now was the time for Eli Sauve.

I puttered down the manicured, palm-lined street, granting the morning armada of power walkers a wide berth. On my first pass, most nodded or waved. But finding green parakeets in green trees required close scrutiny—and more than one pass. Both hands on the wheel, I craned forward to scan the foliage. Nothing could be less nonchalant. By my second and third pass, furrowed brows replaced friendly waves. Dogs strained on their leashes. My driving was too slow and too erratic, and people seemed to be judging whether I was clueless, a predator, or looking for a lost cat. I ignored the looks and noted every mourning dove and mockingbird. Driving down the street wasn't illegal, no matter how many times you do it.

A fourth pass turned up nothing but suspicion. Unwilling to rankle the neighborhood further, I parked my car next to the vacant lot the eBird report noted. Across the canal was the aforementioned feeder. My heart sank: Other than a few scruffy house sparrows, it was equally vacant.

Birdseed, however, is a symbol of hope; I'm a feeder half-full guy. If seed was there, the parakeets would come. The question was: Would they show up before the leery neighborhood watch had my Impala encircled by squad cars? I stepped out of the car and leaned against it, trying way too hard to look casual. Hopefully they'd assume I was an architect scoping out the property specs. No dice. Two bicyclists pedaled up, a man and woman, both trim and silver-haired and looking like spokespeople for longevity supplements. But the fluffy bunny slippers on the woman's feet assured me these two weren't out for a cardio workout. I was the point of their excursion.

"Twitcha?" the man asked.

"Yes, I am a teacher," I replied. "How'd you know?" The woman stifled a laugh.

"No, no, are you a twitcha?" he repeated, his British accent clueing me in.

"A birdwatcher," the woman added, lightly cuffing the man's shoulder.

"Oh, right, yes!" I said, tapping my binoculars.

"Thought so," the man said. "We saw you over tea. That window over there. It's our kitchen."

"I'm looking for rose-ringed parakeets," I said, hoping detail would allay any residual suspicion. "Big green birds that have supposedly been seen around here. I'm on holiday from New York."

"The city?" the woman asked.

"No, the good part," I said, suddenly hoping they didn't also own a flat in Manhattan. "I'm trying to learn about Florida's birds, even though, well, the parakeets aren't really Florida's per se."

"Ya ya," the man said. "You're in the right place. See them every day, from the same window we saw you. We hear them too."

"Crazy loud," the woman added, plucking a pebble from her left bunny.

"Like, annoyingly loud?" I asked.

"Quite," she said, flicking the pebble. "But I'm glad they're here. They add pizzazz."

With a quick "ta-ta," they pedaled off, the bunny's ears on the woman's feet missing the bike's sprockets by millimeters.

"Ta-ta," I mumbled, jealous of their net worth yet charmed by the accent. Clearly, I wasn't the only interloper here: the British couple, the uniformed team of Haitian landscapers down the road, European starlings nesting in the nearby utility pole, the pair of Eurasian collared doves picking their way through the vacant lot, and the rose-ringed parakeets I was after. Immigrants were everywhere, varying only by our place of origin or date of arrival. Who had the right to look down their nose—or bill—at whom?

Immigration is a political hot potato. It's contentious in ecology, too, my discipline of choice. In his 1958 book, *The Ecology of Invasion* by Animals and Plants, ecologist Charles Elton was one of the first to lay crosshairs on nonnative species. Every species, he stated, has a particular niche they've evolved to survive in. Said niches can be thrown asunder by what Elton euphemistically called "dislocations." These, he argued, should be actively resisted and the invaders annihilated, lest ecosystems unravel. Elton, a Brit writing during the height of imperialism, failed to see irony. Or at least he neglected to mention it.

Today in the twenty-first century, there's no such thing as an undisrupted ecosystem. Nanday parakeets, gray-headed swamphens, and legions of others—animals and plants alike—are well established, thriving even. In ecology, the questions have evolved, too. While efforts to remove invasive species persist, attention is shifting to how best to live alongside our new neighbors. What do these species do to ecosystems? How do they interact with the natives? How aggressively do they spread? Do they, like us, have a penchant to plunder and commandeer?

As an ecologist, I've been trained to loathe invasions, regardless of how the invaders arrived. But as I age, I'm leaning into Elton's softer term—dislocations. Afterall, we're responsible for most of these fellow refugees now making the best of their circumstances. Should adaptability be lauded or scorned? Are these maligned invaders merely victims of a global diaspora?

My nativist bias is deep-rooted and hard to dislodge, and I'm not sure I want to. Concepts like "genetic integrity" and "genomic conservation" seem wise to uphold. But Invasion Biology, a recent ecological subdiscipline, makes me nervous. As a few respected biologists remind me, "It is a discipline explicitly devoted to destroying what it studies." When it comes to the naturalized species we live with, humility seems overdue.

—

On Snook Drive, the rose-ringed parakeets were overdue too. Thankfully, before being cross-examined by another Royal Harbor bicycle brigade, they arrived. Three of them cruised overhead and whipped around the feeders like strident boomerangs. One split off, crossed over the canal, and perched atop a flagpole. I raised my binoculars and studied the bird's verdurous palette. Underneath it hung the American flag. Red, white, blue—and green: a nation of immigrants.

I wasn't the only one watching the bird. I heard a door click open three doors down. A blue housecoated woman stepped out. She raised a long-lensed camera, not at me but at the parakeet. The shutter clicked repeatedly. Perhaps this was the first time she'd seen the bird. Or perhaps, like the jogger in Sarasota, she just admired nature for what it was. I reached into my car and pulled out my camera, too. After taking a few shots, we both lowered our lenses and gazed silently upward watching sunlight shimmer off the emerald feathers. Two people, one bird, paying respects to fellow immigrants.

Wildness

The character of being uncultivated, undomesticated, or inhospitable

EURASIAN EAGLE OWL

If only my students paid attention like the homeowners of Royal Harbor. Alas, their limitless anxiety rarely translates to in-class attention. I don't blame them. Who cares about abstract concepts like resource niche partitioning when trying to figure out what to major in and whom—or if—to date or marry. The transition from high school to college is a lot: going from a capacious bedroom and parents filling the gas tank to a closet-sized dorm, a tanked exam, and a gassy roommate. Freshmen struggle with the dizziness of freedom, while upperclassmen face feelings of staleness and captivity.

A Eurasian eagle owl—Flaco—in New York City's Central Park surely felt the latter. Anxious or not, his end was tragic. The story went like this: For all but two of Flaco's fifteen years, he was incarcerated in the Central Park Zoo. Whatever boredom he faced ended abruptly in February, 2023, when vandals, Lord knows why, broke into the zoo and cut a hole in the stainless steel of his enclosure. The event appeared coordinated; zoos across the nation saw other animals break free with assisted escapes. For many of the animals, dizzying freedom proved too much and they returned on their own. Others did not, like the four peacocks that sallied down a Pennsylvanian highway, one colliding with a car.

When Flaco busted out, he didn't give his claustrophobic cubicle a 270-degree glance. Central Park offered a leafy labyrinth he was game to explore. Threats of slavering dogs, kamikaze bicyclists, and rodenticide-laced rats didn't hold a candle to the 842 acres of freedom at his mocha-colored wingtips. The Park, especially the meddlesome jays and crows that protested his presence, wasn't ideal. But it sure beat his cage. If he could survive the raucous days, calmer nights compensated. From a convenient lamppost, he could enjoy the Big Apple's nightlife, especially the overfed and overconfident parade of street rats.

Oh, to return to the old world—sensible, quiet Eurasia! Here, what he lacked in confidants he made up for with superpowers: eyes thirty-five times more sensitive than a person's, ears capable of picking up sounds ten miles away, and sickle-shaped talons that could snuff the life out of squirrel with a slight squeeze. These gifts, coupled with his otherworldly patience, made Central Park suitable—though a far cry from the Siberian forests he preferred. Like a swan goose in corn stubble or a rose-ringed parakeet in Royal Harbor, he would make do.

The silence of a Siberian forest sounds heavenly. Like Flaco, I wouldn't mind a little more peace and quiet. I am an academic. Owlishly introverted, I like to sit and think and stare. But my university is small and my town smaller. In contrast, my students—some of them anyway—have outsized personalities. They come here because they want what larger universities don't offer: to be known. They want regular advising meetings, recommendation letters, and sometimes even, advice on life. I do my best. But when I lose myself in the minutiae, I spring loose from my office, hole up in an overlooked alcove, and gleefully ignore my inbox.

Wired as I am, I've long ignored New York City, too, even though it rises heavenward just a half day's drive away. Flaco changed all that.

Like most New Yorkers, I didn't care about Flaco throughout his incarceration; he was just another inmate stuck in one of the countless zoos and aviaries. But when Flaco broke loose, repeatedly evaded capture, and made a home out of Central Park, I—like so many—couldn't resist. What could be better than a wise old owl making the best of a bad situation? Flaco and I had passed midlife, shared Eurasian roots, and harbored inescapable feelings of entrapment. A cacophonous world swirled about us with a life-altering choice: keep moving or stay put?

Flaco stayed put, but with a caveat: He didn't return to his stage-managed world. He stayed put long enough, in fact, for me to break my students out of their respective cages. It was mid-October, just past the semester's midpoint and high time for a prison break. Eyelids were droopy and classroom walls felt vicelike. Perhaps Flaco could teach us all how to cope with anxiety.

Life on the lam hadn't been easy for the beleaguered owl. For weeks, the Central Park Zoo made every effort to recapture him, resorting to all manner of baits, lures, and snares. Ever so casually, Flaco swooped down, took the bait, and deftly eluded entanglement. Flaco sucked everybody into his orbit like a Shop-Vac—news media, curious onlookers, mushy-hearted animal lovers, and—of course— birders. Paparazzi followed doggedly. Social media erupted. A debate began: Should efforts to recapture him continue? Or had Flaco, having proved he could look after himself, rightfully earned his freedom? What was best for an old, hard-bitten owl: a safer, mundane, boxy life, or the chance to live—and die—as he chose?

Asking myself the same questions, I joined Flaco's freedom cult, my heart lobbying for him to be left alone. Which made my next move remarkably hypocritical: I took my class to go see him. Love for Flaco's story blinded me from this obvious double standard; I should also leave him alone. Instead, with the determination of the Grinch on Christmas Eve, thirteen of my wide-eyed students—most of them country mice like myself—eventually stepped off the Subway onto West 103rd Street.

We immediately met up with Michael, the smiling, in-between-acting-jobs, big-hearted husband of a friend of a sister-in-law who had graciously volunteered to show us about the Park. Michael had fallen for Flaco, too. "I'm not what you would call a birder," he told our group, sweeping an arm toward the calico, autumnal canopy, "but Flaco is irresistible!" Michael paused, eyeing me, and lowered his voice. "Bad news. Nobody has posted his whereabouts today. He may have flown the coop."

My heart hit my shoes. Today was our only day in the Park. Flaco had remained faithfully present for nine straight months. He had withstood torrential rains and whatever hormonal stirrings that still coursed through a middle-aged owl. If Flaco had just departed, it was a profound stroke of bad luck. I glanced at my students. They had heard Michael, but nothing could contain their ebullience. At last they were free. New York City was a big, welcome interruption to their small, routine lives, hardly something the absence of a foreign owl could squelch.

"Owl or not, I'll show you some of my favorite nooks and crannies," Michael said, gesturing down a paved, wooded path. Not long later, Michael pointed into the canopy. "Flaco sat on that sycamore limb for months. Pretty convenient for the throngs of photographers." We all looked up at the stout, horizontal limb, conspicuously bereft of a Eurasian eagle-owl. "I often paid my respects to him here," he said. "Not sure what he liked so much about that tree."

We made several more pitstops, each of them equally owl-less. Out on the outer fringe of the Park's northeast quadrant, the path teemed with a wider lane of go-getters. Rollerbladers and bicyclists wove around joggers, baby strollers, and leashed, happy-go-lucky dogs. "Bummer," Michael said, as we emerged on the park's easternmost edge. "Sure wish I knew where he…wait a…"

I didn't hear the end of Michael's sentence. Rudely, I had left him, crossed the path like Frogger, and power walked up to a handful of serious looking people, most vested and aiming optical equipment upward. Gazes converged on a particular oak. I braced myself; life has taught me that if something is too good to be true, it usually isn't. But axioms don't apply to escaped Eurasian eagle owls in New York

City. In seconds, we had infiltrated the birders, followed their pointing fingers, and found Flaco. On cue, sunbeams broke through the Big Apple haze and bathed the owl in golden light igniting his amber eyes. Accustomed to pint-sized eastern screech owls, Flaco's size immediately impressed me. Flaco means "skinny" in Spanish; if anything, Flaco looked corpulent. Eurasian eagle owls are the second-largest owls in the world. His saucer-sized head was topped with ebony ear tufts, his lethal weaponry neatly concealed under feather duster lower parts. This owl was no rail.

Flaco's passersby seemed frantic beneath his perch. Bicyclists leaned over their handlebars, noticing neither us nor the owl.

The Central Park Zoo, Flaco's old home, was an easy stroll away. The Bronx Zoo, one of the world's most historic, was within easy reach by Subway or Uber. Both places boasted exotic creatures from all over the world—but none that lit up my imagination (or social media) as Flaco did. Flaco hadn't either, when he was in captivity. Our Central Park vigil revealed a truth: A free Eurasian eagle owl is a fundamentally different creature than a caged one. Both eat, poop, and spit up bony pellets, but the captive bird is deprived of possibility, and therefore diminished. Agency made Flaco who he was. Context—place—makes us who we are.

For all that zoos offer in conservation, they lack in context. No matter how detailed and thoughtful the enclosures, animals therein are stripped from life-defining interactions—mates, competitors, predators, prey—that make them who they are. They lose their identity. For all zoos provide physically for animals and educationally for people, they don't—and can't—offer wildness, a concept as elusive as many of the creatures that crave it. "The best zoos can illuminate wildness, but they can never replace it," writes David Quammen. "Wildness is intangible, maybe even ineffable, but not imaginary. It's a matter of size and function and gloriously unpredictable complexity. Religious people might say," he adds, "it's like a soul."

No wonder zoos can't provide such a thing. But they do provide what elephant researcher Iain Douglas-Hamilton refers to as the three

S's: sex, sustenance, and security. Humanity seeks these too. But pursuing these at the expense of wildness comes with a cost. For thirteen years, sustenance and security cost Flaco his wildness. His life became monotonous and diminished. Too much monotony, as my students know from my lectures, can lead to anxiety.

Our twenty-four hours in New York City had caused some anxiety too. Even before we met up with Michael, our country bumpkin roots became obvious. The Subway ticket machine stymied us, we needed officers to manually help us though a turnstile, and we missed a stop because we misinterpreted the train route. Despite towering skyscrapers, we felt exposed and vulnerable, eyes wide and heads craned upward. One of my students, Erica, was especially wary. At the American Museum of Natural History, all of us passed through security without issue. All except her.

"Why did they stop you?" I asked after she'd rejoined our group.

"They made me leave my stuff at the door."

"What stuff?"

"Self-defense stuff," Erica said, eyes not meeting mine.

"Self-defense?" I arched an eyebrow.

"Yeah. Just knives and pepper spray."

"You brought multiple knives?" I asked. She nodded, looking at me with a how-could-you-be-so-naïve face.

"Of course! We're in New York City."

I was annoyed she hadn't informed me about her personal armory, but I didn't fault her; vulnerabilities and misgivings about safety were her business, not mine. How could I blame a student for being cautious? She was a woman with different life experience. Whatever insecurities Erica felt, she hadn't let it prevent her from coming. Perhaps her armaments allowed her to taste the tonic of wildness more completely.

—

No one knows why Flaco made good on his vandal-assisted escape. Was he after wildness? A high-stakes adventure? A lady owl? All three? While I can't understand a captive owl's carnal machinations, I do know this: Just two days after we ogled him in Central Park, Flaco disappeared.

His disappearance sent his fan club into a frenzy. People searched, speculated, and feared the worst. A few anxious days later, he finally showed up in a sculpture garden at the Kenkeleba House Garden. "Hopefully he finds love in East Village," wrote a resident before adding, "We're all looking for love in East Village." Unsurprisingly, Flaco struck out. He was the only Eurasian eagle owl for two thousand miles. And just as suddenly as he'd arrived in the sculpture garden, Flaco returned to Central Park.

Several wise ornithologists speculated that his flight of fancy was indeed hormonally driven. It was breeding season after all, and Flaco was near the end of his reproductive years. It was now or never. His only hope at this point was Geraldine, a fellow resident Central Park owl. But Geraldine was a great horned owl. Could a lovesick Eurasian eagle owl woo a native owl of a completely different species? Would he? Should he? Who who to woo?

We'll never know.

On February 23, 2024, Flaco's inert body was found in a courtyard on West 89th Street. Apparently, he rammed into a building. An autopsy by the Bronx Zoo revealed that his innards were full of rat poison and pigeon virus, a brew that would have killed him even if he had survived the traumatic impact. High toxicity may have caused his final erratic flight.

One of the students from that class graduated the other day and handed me a thank you card. "I had a great time in your class," she wrote. "I may forget the material, but I'll never forget the fun moments, including the trip to NYC and seeing Flaco (may he rest in peace)." She couldn't have said it better: The assignments were forgettable, Flaco wasn't. He isn't.

Flaco was a bird who forged connections with a place he didn't create or choose, a bird who sacrificed convention for a more dynamic life. He may have died in search of wildness. But, unlike so many of us who never break free, Flaco—on the lam for 386 days—really lived.

Indigenous

*Originating or occurring naturally
in a particular place; native.*

G rand as they are, it's probably a good thing Eurasian eagle owls haven't naturalized to New York City. Central Park belongs first to the native owls, to Geraldine and her ilk. My recent fascination with these foreigners, and my efforts to find them, stemmed from relatability; I identify with them. It also stemmed from daily interactions with students who, despite being too young for a midlife crisis, have troubles all their own.

Their crises—both melodramatic and real—stem from daily bouts of soul-searching and a developing understanding of injustice. Stark moments of hope and despair fluctuate unpredictably, sometimes in the middle of class. I envy their idealism, the choices they face, their worlds of possibility. Most have yet to enter the grind, that dark tunnel of unending work that accompanies diaper changes, root canals, knee repairs, forgotten anniversaries, balding, mortgage payments, and neglected gutters which in my case at least, support a miniature tree farm.

With the optimism that comes with spring, the time felt ripe for my Human Ecology course, which explores humanity's relationship to nature, to face some bigger issues. The pandemic was ebbing, birds were singing, and fragile student psyches were stabilizing. But the mood darkened one day in March. "How does climate change make you feel?" I asked blandly, buying time to cue up my slideshow. My students, having long dispensed with formal hand raising, spoke at once.

"Powerless."

"Angry."

"Sad."

"Guilty."

A sea of earnest faces met mine. Outside, sunshine offered a joyful counterpoint. I turned off the projector. "If the planet is warming, we might as well take advantage of it," I said, shutting my laptop. "Grab your stuff. We won't be coming back." I held the door open for them, wondering if my last line doubled as a soon-to-be-fulfilled prophecy for the human race.

Seeking to minimize the sound of campus mowers and potential ambulance sirens, I led my class of twenty-two students to a nearby streamside glade. I eased down onto a patch of pincushion moss and leaned back against a tree, motioning for them to do likewise. A few— the 4-H'ers and homeschooled green thumbs—immediately plopped down. Others frowned, eyeing the forest floor with disdain. I waited. Slowly, they made peace with the dry leaf litter and settled down, one circling like a basset hound on a kitchen floor. Two held out, hovering over the rest of us like suspicious exam proctors, embodying our estranged relationship with planet Earth. A mourning cloak butterfly fluttered weakly by.

Shamelessly self-promotional, I often assign my own books for class discussions. Since I wrote them, I don't have to read them, which frees up time for birding and other forays. This time I had opted for Robin Wall Kimmerer's *Braiding Sweetgrass*. By birthright she is part of the Potawatomi nation. She draws upon these deeply connected roots and contrasts Native American perspectives on the Earth with our more familiar Euro-colonial ones. And Kimmerer is one thing I am not: Indigenous.

Unwilling to spoil the moment with more climate change talk,

I patted my dog-eared copy of the book and asked my second bland question of the day. "What did you all think of today's chapter?"

Before anybody could speak, a yellow-bellied sapsucker strafed our circle, Velcroed itself to a trunk of a cankerous beech, and started drumming. When it paused, Colin—one of my more outspoken students, whose thick dark hair threatened to swallow the pencil he was running through it—broke the reverie. "What do we do?" An undertone of exasperation punctuated his question.

"Do?" I looked at him, confused.

"Yeah. As outsiders without native blood, the author says we can't become Indigenous. So what do we do?"

I chose college teaching because I enjoy honest soul-searching honesty that so often accompanies the late teens-early twenties. Right now, I didn't. I liked raising questions and my favorites were the ones I had answers to.

This one I didn't.

Colin was headed into medicine. In less than two months, he was set to graduate and enter a program that would mold him into a physician's assistant. Up to this point, he had responded to the problems we discussed in class with a redoubt of pat answers. Apparently, climate change, or this book, or some combination thereof, pushed him off balance.

The heavy silence was broken as the sapsucker resumed its drumming. "Did you know," I blurted, "that my daughter Indigo and I counted 2,868 sap wells on a fallen basswood tree the other day?"

"What's a sap well?" Ingrid asked. Ingrid was another question-asker, one who loved nature, especially plants. She had been one of the first to sit down.

"It's a small hole that a sapsucker drills. The tree responds to the injury by coating it with sticky sap which, in turn, attracts insects. Several times a day, the bird visits its traplines for both the sap and the insects."

Ingrid nodded and laid all the way down on her back.

"Twenty-eight hundred isn't all that many," I said. "Other ecologists have counted eighty thousand. On a single tree." Nobody spoke. They were either awestruck or eager to return to Colin's question. I guessed the latter—but, to me, bird data was vital. It wasn't just that these factoids hung in my brain like stalactites, while more relevant info like committee meeting dates, leaked away. Birds had answers. They were answers. How birds responded to the questions of life surely had lessons for the rest of us. "The yellow-bellied sapsucker migrates further than the other sapsuckers," I finished, conscious that I'd neglected to mention a disconcerting addendum that they were arriving earlier and earlier each spring.

More silence.

"I found the spot," Colin said, his copy of *Sweetgrass* open. "Can I just read it?"

"Sure."

Colin read.

"Like my elders before me, I want to envision a way that an immigrant society could become Indigenous to place, but I'm stumbling on the words. Immigrants cannot by definition be Indigenous. Indigenous is a birthright word. No amount of time or caring changes history or substitutes for deep-soul fusion with the land."

"See what I mean?" Colin said. "I'm not Indigenous nor can I become so."

I startled at how Colin personalized his remark this time. "None of us are." Heads nodded affirmingly. "So what do we do?" he asked, changing the pronoun to include us all.

"If we can't be Indigenous, what can we be?" I asked. I was thinking back to my recent time in Florida, watching gloriously green immigrant parakeets brighten the sky.

"She says we have to naturalize," Colin said, thumbing through his book. "I underlined it."

"I love that part," flannel-shirted Zoe interjected. "Don't think I'm weird, but I actually read that section to my mother over the phone. I have it marked, too. 'Being naturalized to place means to live as if this is the land that feeds you,'" Zoe read, "'as if these are the streams from which you drink, that build your body and fill your spirit.'"

It was a typical class discussion: a small handful of students carrying the load for the more reticent, silently thanked by those who hadn't cracked the book. But the others were listening. One of the hoverers had rolled a rock over to sit on. One by one, connections were forming.

"So what's wrong with being naturalized?" I asked, looking at Colin. Before he could answer, Ingrid, still staring up at the canopy from her supine position, spoke up.

"I think we're just overthinking it." More heads nodded. The discussion continued, flowing like the stream's water beside us.

We were surely overthinking it, but this was college. If anything, our colonial heritage leads us to underthink our relationship to nature, hence the many environmental problems we spent weeks discussing. Like most of my classes, the conversation lurched to an ungainly stop when three o'clock hit, and people reflexively started gathering their belongings. I left the loose ends untied, announced the next reading assignment, and the class ended.

I trailed my students out of the woods as they split up for the daily regimen of afternoon classes, sports practices, and instrument lessons. Many of them, soon-to-be graduates, I'd forever lose track of. I might never know if Colin would one day find satisfactory answers to the questions he raised. In a blink, he'd be a physician's assistant working long hours. More likely than not, he'd pair up, raise children, take out a mortgage, and settle. Would he experience soul-fusion with the land? Would he naturalize? Would any of this matter?

The good part about being a professor: That coming summer, I'd have a chance to hang out with another group of earnest students, this time at the Au Sable Institute of Environmental Studies, in Michigan.

The course and the context would change, but the all-important question would remain: How do we forge a deeper identity with the land?

Behind me, the sapsucker's drumbeat slowed. Try as I might to match the bird's rhythm with my stride, I remained out of step.

Wilderness

An uncultivated, uninhabited, and inhospitable region.

COMMON LOON

"

W hat is the trouble with wilderness?" I asked Esther. She cringed. "I can tell you what the trouble with my brain is," she said. "It doesn't know the answer."

"Clever. Just read whatever you wrote."

"According to William Cronon," Esther read, "the trouble with wilderness is that it's hard to define."

"A decent starting point," I remarked. "Anyone else?"

Hannah, a Sustainability and Communication double major, raised her hand. "Wilderness is a human construct," she read, "a concept we've made up."

"And," Micah chimed in, "how we've viewed wilderness has changed a lot."

"How?" I asked, encouraged I no longer had to call on people. This group of ten students from a host of different universities were all environmentally-minded; once the engine was revved, they rolled.

"Cronon kept calling it a howling wilderness, something people wanted to tame," Lizzy said. "But Muir called it sacred and the attitude shifted to preservation."

"Not everybody's attitude," Micah interrupted.

Lizzy rolled her eyes.

"Obviously."

"So what is the general attitude now? What do you think, Jake?" Unlike the others, Jake rarely spoke unless called upon. He had his sights set on urban planning, something his uncle did, while the others were interested in wildlife rehabilitation and ecological restoration in more remote and natural settings. Knowing precious little about urban planning I couldn't resist teasing him about his environmental future amid a sea of skyscrapers and concrete. Sitting on a stump in the minimally altered forest of Au Sable Institute's campus, Jake stared off into the lower branches of a white pine.

"I think it's a mix," he finally said. "Some see the importance of wilderness. Others not so much." Heads nodded.

Though the students technically had an hour left of class, I didn't. I had three hundred miles to drive that evening, a tent to set up that night, and a plane to catch early the next morning. The conservation biology course was more than half over. With four days until our next scheduled class, I had studied the map of Michigan, calculated travel times, and impulsively booked a floatplane. An island forty-five miles long and nine miles wide—Isle Royale National Park—beckoned me with open arms from the middle of Lake Superior. It was one of the least visited national parks, attracting fewer people per year than Yellowstone typically gets in a day. Isle Royale boasted moose, wolves, and loons. My arrival would increase this latter population by one.

"So," I said, stealing a nervous glance at my watch, "would Cronon call this place—this ring of stumps right here—wilderness?" I looked around. Nobody spoke. Jake stared blankly at his feet. Esther prodded the dirt with a stick. Hannah twirled a leaf. For whatever reason, the class had morphed into a deflated party balloon.

For three straight weeks, I had bombarded them with abstruse concepts, assignments, and readings. Perhaps this last one had broken the camel's back, but it was too important to let slide. "Claire, you've got a fifty–fifty shot. Is this place wilderness?"

Just one year out of high school, Claire was even more reserved than Jake. Her freckled complexion turned scarlet as she nodded hesitantly. "Care to elaborate?" I asked, my competing desires to drive the point home and start my journey north blending into unconcealed passive aggressiveness.

"I didn't quite finish the reading," Claire admitted, running her fingers through a fern. Too annoyed to let her off the hook, I remained quiet, expectant. Finally, she broke the silence. "Cronon didn't separate people from wilderness. So, in that sense, this place is wilderness."

"But we're here," I challenged. "These buildings, electrical lines, sewer pipes. Doesn't all this stuff—the infrastructure—nullify wilderness?"

Still fiddling with her fern, Claire shook her head.

For dramatic effect, my seventh-grade social studies teacher, Mr. Burt, used to stand on a chair and write across the wall when he ran out of chalkboard. In honor of beloved Mr. Burt, I leapt onto my stump.

"Exactly!" Heads popped up and eyes widened. Mission accomplished. "That's what Cronon meant! Micah, will you read his words on page four, second paragraph." Micah flipped through his packet, finger coming to rest halfway down the page.

"The trouble with wilderness is that it quietly expresses and reproduces the very values its devotees seek to reject," Micah read. I cut him off and snapped a twig off an overhanging hemlock.

"Underline that," I ordered, waving my crude conducting baton. "Cronon is saying that we fashioned wilderness into a place where we aren't." I paused. "Hence the trouble."

Silence. "Can I have an amen?" Crickets.

"Wait, so why is that troubling?" Hannah asked. I stared at her incredulously. Her confusion killed my Mr. Burt impersonation.

"People live everywhere, right?" I asked.

"Not totally everywhere."

"Yes we do!" I protested. "Have you ever flown across the US and seen the mosaic of rectangles butting up one against each other? The never-ending ag fields?"

"Yeah."

"We're not everywhere, but we've appropriated a lot," I said. "So what does that mean for wilderness?"

"It means there can't be any," Hannah said.

Micah saw where I was going and closed the loop. "Right, if we only value and protect wilderness but define it as wherever we aren't, we won't protect the places we live."

"Cronon couldn't have said it better," I said, nearly losing my balance as the stump teetered under me like an unsteady top.

"He certainly could have said it more concisely," Esther said. She rolled up her packet, signaling her participation was done.

"If you remember nothing else from this course," I said as I jumped down, "every scrap counts. This campus. Your yard. The swampy ditch beside the gas station. It may not feel like wilderness. But to the sowbug, the robin, the leopard frog, these places do. Wilderness abounds. The concept depends on perspective."

I halted my monologue, hoping silence would drive it home. It didn't. Cronon's ideas impacted me viscerally, not so my students. Only Jake—the urban planner—was moving his pen, though more likely sketching his shoe than recording my words. Late June's mugginess had conquered the class. I raised the white flag and gathered my stuff. These students wanted to swim, not reconceptualize wilderness. So be it. Punitively, I handed out another reading and headed for my already packed car.

With four days of freedom ahead, not even a dead discussion could wipe out my smile. it was just me and my Kia Sorento, cruising north toward the Mackinac Bridge. No small talk, no fights over AC, and no bathroom breaks, just the way I liked it. My students would surely ignore the reading, and I would ignore the stack of ungraded papers and an inbox full of requests.

One night and one footlong Subway sandwich later, I stepped off a floatplane onto a dock on Isle Royale's Tobin Harbor. I had a duffle bag, a fishing pole, and binoculars—all one needs for a hot date with an island. I strode up the path with a few others and quickly secured a screened lean-to, tucked between bracken fern and scraggily spruce trees, the screen to keep out the bird-sized mosquitoes that would arrive at dusk. Graffiti—carved or written with a Sharpie—adorned the rough-hewn walls. Most was the typical "I'm sick of granola" hiker sentiment. But others marked more meaningful rites of passage:

Joshua and Dad
Father-son trip
Josh is 5
Walked 30 miles

The oddest line appeared over my head, boldly burnt into a cross-beam: "If you can read this, don't thank a prostitute."

Time didn't allow for a thru-hike, but it did allow for thorough exploration of my tip of the island. Stoll Point was Isle Royale's easternmost terminus. With that as my goal, I slung on a day pack, grabbed my fishing pole, and set off.

The hike had everything: cool breezes off Lake Superior, dainty flowers, and piles of moose scat which bore an uncanny resemblance to unwrapped Tootsie Rolls. Cinnamon-colored hares eyed me from the underbrush, their blindingly white feet having yet to get the memo that summer was at hand. Born with an inability to resist interpretative signs, I stopped to read one entitled: "Stoll's Wilderness."

"Beyond here you enter designated wilderness. You will find no more signs that explain what you see. The purpose of designated wilderness is to retain a primeval character, with the imprint of humans substantially diminished. Beyond this point you must make your own discoveries."

Brow furrowed, I read the sign again. Hadn't I been making my own discoveries the whole time? What did interpretive signs have to do with wilderness? Did their presence in a place negate its presence? Had Isle Royale's staff fallen for such an obvious false dichotomy? Why were they overtly perpetuating the trouble with wilderness? Had they not read Cronon's piece?

One thing I did know: I wouldn't find answers to these questions on any more park signs.

I couldn't fault the sign maker's intention: In some places, we should do our utmost to minimize the markings of humanity. But the implication was unsettling. It meant that the previous hour I'd spent hiking to this spot—edging around beaver ponds, photographing flowers, spying for glimpses of lupine movement in the shadows—had happened in a non-wilderness place, a lesser environment. If humanity sullied a landscape, my presence here compounded the problem; every step I took further spoiled the wilderness's primeval character.

Answers eluded me, but a family of loons didn't. On the way back from Stoll Point, while skirting a tranquil bend in Tobin Harbor, two large loons paddled a stone's throw from shore. Between them, bobbing about, were two fluffy, black chicks—loonlets—each the size and shape of a grapefruit. Eager to watch, I settled amid some lowbush blueberry, an ideal harborside seat.

The loons, perhaps recognizing me as one of their own, went about their loony business peaceably. While one parent fussed over the chicks, the other dove and reemerged with a shiny, pinky-sized fish. The sight of the wriggling fish sent the chicks into a frenzied race. While the winner grappled with the prize, the petulant loser soon received another fish from the other parent. One fish, two fish, me fish, you fish.

Untold fish later, the chicks clambered onto the back of a parent, temporarily sated. An indelible scene, two smudgy, snuggly balls of dryer lint nestled atop a striking parent. To the scientists, here was *Gavia immer*—the ash-colored smew. To the Brits, the great northern diver. My field guide called them common loons, which I accepted until really getting to watch these mystical birds.

Etymologists can't pinpoint where "loon" comes from. Probably from the Old English word "lumme," for an awkward person, or the Scandinavian word "lum," implying clumsiness. If you watch loons lumber about on land with their legs positioned aft, the associations are apt; they'd be hard-pressed to out waddle a slinky. Loons know this. They also know the Earth is 71 percent water, which makes much of the world their oyster.

On the water, the great northern diver is great. Under the water, it's even greater. Using its back legs as jet propulsion, the loon's solid bones allow it to reach depths of two hundred feet where it can remain for up to five minutes. When its cupboard freezes over in the autumn, the loon sprints across the surface and flaps. Its wings become airfoils urgently slicing them through the air at seventy miles per hour. As the loon gradually gains altitude, the waterbody below shrinks into a sentence-ending period.

Loons move from lake to lake in dry-cleaned tuxedos. They have conceded the color palette to wood ducks but compensated with elegance and crisp, checkerspot attire. Their ruby red eyes help them filter light when feeding in murky depths and shoot down Jedi X-wing fighters when aloft.

Mere waterfront property doesn't cut it for the loon. It nests on islands well away from the hoi polloi, the more desolate the better. If islands are booked, floating mats of vegetation suffice. In this liminal world, well away from marauding mink and ravenous raccoons, the female lays two gray-brown eggs. The precocious young take to the water quickly. Parental piggybacking reduces their vulnerability to northern pike and opportunistic snapping turtles.

Adept, exquisite, doting, and most memorably: musical. At dawn, through an ethereal mist, the loon unleashes a tremolo that infiltrates the marrow of my bones. It is, writes John McPhee, "the laugh of the deeply insane." Then, if its loonlets are in a row, the bird wails, a soul-rending cry that sends a shiver up my spine. Whatever I'm doing stops. Chin out, my gaze settles into the gray middle distance.

Terrible nomenclature, there is nothing common about the loon. They do these things. They are these things. Pacific loons, Arctic loons, yellow-billed loons, red-throated loons—all five share these qualities. But common loons are my loons. On boyhood backcountry Adirondack camping trips, I awoke to their haunting melodies; the great northern diver imprinted on my soul. Loons are not the trouble with wilderness; they embody it.

Names matter. The French knew this; "Isle Royale," sounds like a James Bond movie. Since James Bond was named after a birder, and his creator Ian Fleming also wrote *Birds of the West Indies*, the name fits. The point is, had the French called it "Le Lieu des Moustiques," "the place of mosquitoes," it may have never garnered enough attention to be elevated to a national park. The cool name, and National Park status, lent cachet.

While the name stuck, the French were hardly the first to witness the royal island's significance. Indigenous peoples beat them by a long shot, some forty-five hundred years earlier, an unknown number of people paddled over and christened it "Minong," "the good place." Later, the Algonquin-speaking Ojibwa—the Anishinaabe—hunted and collected copper, which they fashioned into arrowheads, knives, and other sought-after items.

When the French fur trappers finally arrived, the island became a convenient stopping place for rest—and exploitation. Goods were sent east along the Great Lakes conveyor belt. Isle Royale remained like this—a useful commons—until it fell under American control via a sad debacle of sham treaties and political sleight-of-hand. By the mid-nineteenth century, the good place was "owned."

Good as it was, the buggy isle escaped the fawning attention that many other, more convenient islands, received. For decades, the island was used by fishermen, artists, and a handful of hardy vacationers. Had it not, it might easily have succumbed to the fate of Mackinac Island, where people go for fudge, horse carriage rides, and a slew of other forgettable tchotchkes.

Without consumeristic bipeds bustling about, quadrupeds moved in. During cold winters, when ice formed a land bridge between Ontario and Isle Royale, a parade of courageous creatures made landfall, headlined by moose and wolves. A handful of savvy scientists showed up not long later, eager to study colonization, dispersal, and predator-prey dynamics. For the gleeful scientists, the surrounding moat simplified the island, turning it into a bounded laboratory. At last count, Isle Royale had nineteen mammals, less than half the faunal cast in nearby Ontario. Fewer species made ecological relationships more decipherable; gone were so many pesky, conflating variables, not to mention wilderness's sticking point: human presence.

For a bird's eye perspective of the island, I spent the next day perched atop Mount Franklin. From there, I gazed out over Lake Superior, spying hazy Canada to the north. Isle Royale, I quickly realized, was much more than one royal island. Lakes covered the island, many boasting smaller islands of their own, akin to the Matryoshka dolls that nest one inside the other. While I could see just a few, an eye-popping 450 smaller islands dotted the waterscape.

The good place stood in stark contrast to America's quickly-becoming-bad places: most everywhere else that didn't require a long boat ride or a float plane to reach. Sensing this, Herbert Hoover authorized Isle Royale in order "to conserve a prime example of North Woods wilderness." With the Wilderness Act of 1964, Lyndon B. Johnson went a step farther. With the stroke of Johnson's pen, nine million acres were preserved for their "original and unchanging beauty and wonder." Around this time, David Brower, president of the Sierra Club, went before lawmakers. "Wilderness lets a place have a beyond to it," he told them. "It symbolizes the freedom to choose what kind of terrain you want to look at, or hope someday to enter, or to save for your children to enter. Without it the world is a cage." Not quite a Flaco-sized cage, but Brower's point was clear: Wilderness had sprung free.

Wilderness fandom became as cultish as Flaco's. "In wildness,"

Thoreau wrote in his essay, "Walking is the preservation of the world." Wildness, not wilderness. Yet disciples of untouched wilderness readily tweaked wildness to their ends. The line often remains misquoted today. It's a sad fact. Wildness and wilderness are different concepts, I habitually tell my students. Wildness is a state of being, wilderness a place. Wildness can come about in wilderness, but not the other way around.

Jumbled or not, wilderness had come to roost in the American conscience. Out of it grew the National Wilderness Preservation System, a vast network of more than eight hundred designated wilderness units amounting to 111 million acres, managed by four federal agencies. Some, like Wrangell-St. Elias's nine million acres, are incomprehensibly large. Others, like the Rocks and Islands Wilderness Area, along California's northern coastline, are just a smidge larger than my three-acre yard.

I adore this size range; wilderness mustn't be huge. I likewise adore the Act's definition of wilderness, partly because it sounds like Shakespeare wrote it: "a place where the earth and its community of life are untrammeled by man."

"Trammel," which I had to look up, means "to deprive of freedom and action." Had I, while watching the loons from my carpet of moss, trammeled them? It didn't seem so. But I did know this: All 111 million acres amounted to just two percent of the Lower 48. Wilderness preservation didn't—it doesn't—mean squat if we're trammeling the other 98 percent.

Today's students may be social media dependent and distracted, but they're not dumb. Furthermore, they're wolflike when they catch a whiff of hypocrisy. And when I arrived back the following week from my Isle Royale sojourn, I reeked of it. Micah, the most outspoken, called me out. "You mean you drove six hours north and then boarded a floatplane?" he asked sardonically. What's wrong with the wilderness right here?"

Guilty as charged; a defense was useless. I was obviously the trouble with wilderness. I was also supercharged from my experience in the 2 percent. For the next ten minutes, I drowned my students with passionate, run-on sentences about the moose browsing outside my lean-to, the phantasmagoric sunsets, and of course, the cute little loonlets and the loon music that lulled me to sleep. I even told them about a few people I met, all fascinating and respectful, who enhanced my experience rather than sullied it. A crazy thought: fellow animals—people—augmenting wilderness rather than reducing it.

When I came up for air, Lizzy tempered Micah's ribbing: "I so want to go there," she whispered. I hope she does. This is the beauty of the two percent, from six-acre Rock Island to nine-million-acre Wrangell-St. Elias. They exist to inspire us, to encourage us. They are what the other 98 percent can be if we revere all the sacred ground—and water—around us.

Naturally, the great northern diver breeds in the north. But the tuxedoed, laser-eyed loon passes through all the Lower 48; we can see them anywhere. The loon knows the value of the 98 percent; its life depends on it. Vital knowledge which makes the bird, to me at least, remarkably uncommon.

Consanguineous

Of the same blood or origin

WHITEBREASTED
NUTHATCH

Only a brother can make me loathe fall migration. One innocuous question sent over our family's group chat began my angsty autumn: "Is it common to see bluebirds in March?" How I answered that question isn't important. What is important, at least in the brood I was reared with, is who's on top. My brother Andrew's bird list for his pretty average yard in the outskirts of Grand Rapids, Michigan, stands at 124 species: pretty decent. A better sibling, a better man, would laud this impressive haul, complete with bald eagles, a leucistic blue jay, and a recent pair of roosting long-eared owls, that lured in a parliament of camera-wielding acolytes. But I can't. Whatever happiness I feel is edged with sibling rivalry, manifesting in acreage rivalry. I am a lesser man.

I am also a man itching for indigeneity, or at least to naturalize the best I can. Isle Royale floatplanes are expensive; I want wildness in all its forms, to embrace the wilderness that extends out my back door. To heed Albert Einstein's advice and "widen my circle of compassion and embrace all living creatures and the whole of nature in its beauty." Ultimately, I want to cultivate my own royal island.

Nascent sibling rivalry aside, I was still embracing Andrew with sibling compassion. "I'm up to twenty-one birds for my yard!" he declared proudly, attaching a blurry photo of a starling to his text. My compassionate smile widened with his next question: "How many different species have you seen in your yard?"

My thumbs couldn't text fast enough. I had grown up as a lone birder in a family of six. Could it be? Was somebody I shared DNA with really interested in nonhuman life? I had waited my whole life for this. Better yet, I had obsessively recorded every species that had perched or flown over my quotidian three-acre lot in western New York. The idea hatched when I spied a Carolina wren poking around my garage while sorting recyclables. The wren was more interested in the surprised spiders than me. How many other birds do I share my space with, I idly wondered. I went inside and taped a piece of paper to the inside door of our pantry. Uncreatively across the top I wrote: "Birds Seen in Yard," with the record of the Carolina wren underneath. My list grew quickly after that, expanding into additional categories for "flyovers," "nesting birds," and birds I "heard only."

The endeavor was very much in character; lists have plagued me since the days I recorded "good birds" and "bad birds" at my home-made feeders that I'd watch by the hour from the faded cushions of our bay window. My categories were merely skin deep. Bad birds were bullies: jays, red-winged blackbirds, and worst of all, the greasy grackles that often tipped my poorly made feeders over and spilled the seed. Good birds were dainty and demure: goldfinches, chickadees, and the occasional—and much longed for—indigo bunting.

I didn't realize it then but birds were a metaphor. The world was competitive and I—third in the line of four—wasn't sure how to compete. I lacked the novelty of the oldest and the fawning that the youngest—Andrew—received. While my siblings played Atari and Nintendo, I built feeders and hunted rabbits. While they read Tolkien, I flipped through field guides. I felt weird for liking birds and often wished for mainstream interests. There I was under the feeder, a nondescript sparrow scratching for seed, while more colorful beings flew about overhead.

Andrew's birding inquiry changed all that. He validated me; at long last, a family member understood.

Ninety-seven birds, I zealously typed back, attaching a photo of my list, still faithfully hanging on the back of the pantry door. After the wren, I'd padded my list with A-listers like Louisiana waterthrush, black-billed cuckoo, and common nighthawk. It became a game: How many birds could I lure in by making it more bird-friendly? I hand dug pitiful ponds, built-up monstrous brush piles, and let dead trees stand as long as they didn't threaten to knock out a child. Plant-by-plant and bird-by-bird, my little postage stamp of property was wrapping tendrils around my soul. For them and for me, symbiosis, habitat creation was a labor of love.

When young Charles Darwin sent impassioned letters home to his sister during his five-year odyssey on the voyage of the Beagle, she replied with a list of spelling errors that he'd made. Andrew was similarly minded. If he was impressed with my list, he didn't show it. "You double counted Northern Flicker," he wrote back immediately. "And how, pray tell, have you not seen an American crow?"

Whoops. I had seen an American crow, of course. That very morning, in fact, along with a common raven. The previous summer I had nearly mowed over a baby crow that had tumbled from a nest on my yard's border. For what it's worth: Unless you want the fury of the avian gods unleashed upon you, do not, I repeat, do not, move a baby crow. The point is, crows were so common and I so obtuse that I'd failed to add them to my list. Hmph. Only a brother can make me loathe bird listing.

Over the next few months, Andrew's texts kept coming. More surprisingly, he started calling too. Even more surprising—inveterately phone averse—I started answering. Never had we communicated this much. But there was so much to talk about. "I saw this bird," he'd begin, or: "You'll never believe what just flew over my yard." As his experience grew, his questions morphed into confident statements. "Blue-headed vireo," he wrote one day, following it the next day with: "Red-headed woodpecker." When his list climbed into the sixties, he reverted to a question: "What kind of camera would you recommend?"

Andrew was hardly the first person I'd seen hit with the bird bug. The field ornithology courses I taught, which required students to watch and list, had accrued a respectable list of converts. We studied American birds, and often went overseas. Some caught it under the spell of blue-crowned motmots and resplendent quetzals. Others while spying their first yellow warbler, a bird who had escaped their notice despite sharing a backyard. But Andrew's conversion was different. He was naturalizing, focusing on the immediate, and discovering the wilderness of his yard. This was a consanguineal conversion; Andrew was flesh and blood.

It had another twist: Andrew was cut of the same competitive cloth I was. He had OCD tendencies, a sharp eye, and his land abutted the Grand River, which transformed his land every spring into a seasonal wetland, a hotspot for birds my yard could never attract. Andrew's list was growing exponentially, mine had long since flatlined. Smelling blood, he sensed my list was on life support.

In the midst of our competition, Andrew paid me a visit. "Here is my path to one hundred," he said as we sat outside on my deck. "This fall, I expect winter wren, yellow-rumped warbler, fox sparrow..."

"Check out that white-breasted nuthatch," I happily interrupted, pointing to the dapper little bird ratcheting down a nearby pine. The nuthatch held his head perpendicular to his downward facing body, as if held by a neck brace. I didn't want to hear his path to one hundred. That would take his list a few birds past mine; I would be beaten and rankled.

"I get tons of those," Andrew said. "But I can't get a red-breasted nuthatch for the life of me."

ANK-ANK! The nuthatch responded, flying off to another tree. "ANK" happened to be Andrew's initials. Only a nuthatch could ruin a lovely afternoon.

In a more meaningful way, Andrew and the nuthatch made the day special. Here we were, sitting outside with binoculars, talking birds. For the first time in my life, I was reveling in an interest with a family member, an interest so deep it had shaped my career. We were sharing it. We were just being brothers—meddlesome and competitive cheer-leaders yoked together with common history and familial love. Plus, Andrew hadn't beaten me yet. I had hope. Maybe his path to one hundred would get foiled. Birds weren't electrons. They had brains, wills, and unpredictability. Hopefully they'd use those brains to skip over my brother's yard on their south-bound journeys. Maybe, Grinchian smile spread across my face, the green herons and osprey he planned for would choose other waters to ply. Maybe the avian gods would smite his yard and plateau it—wicked cackle—at an eternal eighty species.

Andrew's ardor spurred me on. I redoubled my efforts at habitat creation. I dammed my creek, piled brush higher, and religiously topped up my feeders. Alas, all Sisyphean.

"The path of freezing water is predetermined," tech philosopher Kevin Kelly wrote. "But there is great leeway, freedom, and beauty in the individual expression of its predetermined state." Andrew's list passed mine. Then it plateaued, after that stupid pair of long-eared owls gave him a double-digit lead. I'll need the fallout of my life to recover it.

But Andrew's newfound love of birds has had a deeper, more meaningful fallout. Not long ago, it seemed predetermined that he would live out his days not caring a whit about nature. Now, he notices, records, and communicates. He cares. The closer our lists have gotten, the closer we have gotten. This is the great leeway, the freedom and beauty of a predetermined state. Our biodiversity contest is remarkably trivial, our relationship anything but.

Fall migration was good to him. Andrew's predicted path to one hundred proved robust. Even birds he didn't predict dropped in on him: magnolia warbler, black-and-white warbler, Tennessee warbler, and even—like he predicted—an obliging winter wren. His wilderness proved a worthy rest stop for the multitudes. Which means that I've never been happier to see this transitory time of massive bird movement cease. Winter, make haste! Only a brother can make me loathe fall migration.

Navigation

*The process or activity
of accurately ascertaining
one's position and planning
and following a route.*

Sibling journeys are Clematis vines climbing up a trellis. They arise from a common seed and branch off in different directions, each shoot seeking growth and opportunity. Some tendrils get further and further apart. Others, due to dead ends or new discoveries, spiral back toward one another.

My three siblings and I all sprouted from a wordy seed, one predicated on predicates, prepositions, and all manner of wordplay. Of the four of us, Andrew's recent conversion into the bird world had extended my love—and occasional abuse—of metaphor. If consanguineal journeys are Clematis vines, then humanity is the southern lapwing.

The national bird of Uruguay is the southern lapwing, too, which made it odd when a lone lapwing touched down on the unkempt grass adjoining a runway at Michigan's small Oscoda-Wurtsmith Airport on Lake Huron's western shore this past June. Southern lapwings are aptly named; they are elegant, long-legged birds that breed in Central and South America, rarely showing interest in the Northern hemisphere. When I recently checked eBird, nobody had seen a southern lapwing in the US prior to 2006. That made a southern lapwing falling in Michigan as likely as snow falling in the Florida keys; seeing one myself akin to skiing on it.

Though snow was far my mind, I did happen to be in Michigan's mitten, fresh back from Isle Royale and the end of my Conservation Biology course. With spring migration long over, my brother Andrew took a break from militant yard surveillance and drove his family up from Grand Rapids so we could spend some together. By the time we dumped our duffles into a rental house, eBird-ing Andrew had already caught wind of the hemisphere-defying lapwing. Just an hour away, I didn't need convincing.

Two mornings later, Andrew, Ezra, and I pulled into the little-used airport, a depressing place for an all-star bird. Tired jetliners, their company names peeling off their tail fins, lined one end. In the middle was a cluster of dull, shoebox-shaped buildings and cavernous hangars, guarded by chain-link and razor wire. The dark and threatening sky heightened the apocalyptic feel. If we laid eyes on the lapwing, this overcast penitentiary would rank up there with the Ecuadorian dump that had bequeathed burrowing owls and the Viera sewage plant where I'd spied my first purple gallinule.

"Over there," Andrew said, pointing to a line of six small sedans, all looking like run-of-the-mill rentals. I pulled behind the last car, and we hastily clambered out, fearful the lapwing had suddenly realized its thousand-odd mile gaffe. Like a low budget picket line, A loose gaggle of hunched over people stood behind mounted lenses, pressed as close to the chain link as possible.

"Is it still here?" I asked the first man I came to. In diehard birding circles, pleasantries are secondary to the immediacy of a bird's presence. He looked up from his scope, adjusted his plaid fly cap, and smiled.

"Have a look," he said, pointing at his scope. My heart raced as the dapper lapwing came into focus. Crisp black-and-white front: Check. Sandy back: Check. Red pencil legs: Check. Feathered plume off the back of the head: check. Southern lapwing indeed.

"Unbelievable," I said, prying myself from the eyepiece so Andrew and Ezra could have a look.

"Tell me about it," he said. "First US record."

"Seriously?"

"Well, first documented sighting. There's an iffy record fifteen years ago in Maryland. And maybe one from Florida." I nodded, basking in the arbitrary glory that accompanies paying witness to odd phenomena.

"Where are you from?" I asked, impressed with his mental record of minutiae.

"Flew in from Houston yesterday."

"Houston?" I didn't mention that our rental house was fortuitously an hour away.

"No way I was missing this bird." He continued. "It's nothing compared to what I had to do for Steller's sea eagle. Two flights to Alaska.

"Two?"

"First time I missed it because I was on the wrong side of the helicopter. Still sore about that one. Then again, that's the fun of it all. Compared to that, this bird's a slam dunk."

I made my way slowly down the line, sharing similar banter with all the lapwing watchers. All were equal parts amiable and demented, though none as extreme as the wrong-side-of-the-helicopter guy. "Given time you will eventually match your own habits, at home and afield, to the habits of the animal you study," Ellen Meloy writes. "Bird-watchers rise at dawn, peck at little plates of seeds and raisins, do their errands in eager swoops." Meloy's words make me cringe. Paying attention to small things overlooked by the world feels right. But is worth forfeiture of time, money, and sleep? Not to mention the carbon we spew into the atmosphere while out on our quests. To what lengths should I go for foreign little vagrants statuesque in the grass?

Mowed grass, that is. At that very moment, a zero-turn mower zoomed around a building with obvious designs on the lapwing's patch. "You guys might have arrived in the nick of time," said a lady in a tan, many-pocketed, vest. "Hope this isn't the coup de grace!"

I followed the mower in my binoculars. The man atop it wore

unnecessary sunglasses and massive blaze-orange earphones. He appeared not to notice the bird or understand its significance. Trapped behind the fence, we were powerless to intervene. Nervous silence ensued. If the bird didn't move now, the mower would churn out lapwing confetti.

Avian nonchalance, the lapwing seemed to view the obstreperous mower like one of the gormless cows it chewed the fat with down in Peru. When the mower rumbled up behind, the lapwing sidestepped like an experienced matador. With little more than a few wingbeats, the gracile bird resumed its vigil on the lawn. Grass now uniform, the mower beelined for unrulier pastures.

My students and I had just wrapped up a month zooming around Michigan, learning from people in state parks, fish hatcheries, and nature sanctuaries. We had discussed habitat destruction, land use, resource exploitation, and Cronon's concept of wilderness. Metaphorically the mower was apt. It symbolized humanity's fraught relationship with nature, its mindless pursuit of control. In place after place, ecosystems were tamed, growth arrested. But leaning against the fence, fingers through the chain link, a much different metaphor appeared. Perhaps we were—we are—the lapwing?

Our wings have taken us far. But is it where we want to be? Can we make it back? Should we even try?

Official bird records are funny things. Even if multiple witnesses document a bird's presence in a new place, the record doesn't automatically become sacrosanct. Records have record committees. They are decidedly democratic processes; a cadre of vetted people vote based upon all available evidence and research. For the southern lapwing to officially become the first North American record, it first had to be affirmed as having arrived on its own accord. Unlike Flaco and the raucous rabble of Floridian parakeets, the lapwing couldn't be an escapee, assisted or otherwise.

As bird cases go, the lapwing's was pretty sound. Foul play (ahem) wasn't suspected. Its wings weren't clipped nor were its legs banded. No distraught pet owner was searching for a lost lapwing nor had any aviary revealed that any were unaccounted for. And yet, nobody could account for its arrival either. So the matter went to a vote. In a 5–2 ruling, the Michigan Bird Records Committee affirmed the lapwing arrived on its accord. The American Birding Association—the ABA for short—quickly followed suit and the southern lapwing, *Vanellus chilensis*, was added to the ABA checklist as an "accidental species from other regions that are believed to have strayed here unrestrained by humans."

A local birder and photographer, Jason Shaw, visited the lapwing throughout its six-month stay in eastern Michigan. "The evidence gathered by people vastly outweighed the initial thought of it being a stowaway on a plane," Shaw stated. "There is too much evidence to support the wild bird decision."

I'm glad the lapwing was added both locally and nationally. And yet I can't help but wonder about those two early dissenting votes among the Michigan Bird Records Committee. What did the two nay-sayers know that the others didn't? Were they waiting for somebody to come forward? Or were they just skeptical that a bird that rarely strayed further north than Guatemala and Belize would make such a profound navigational blunder?

I don't doubt any creature's ability to blunder. But I do sometimes doubt the ability to correct a bad one. As the winds turned icy off Lake Huron in late December, the lapwing might have tried. Come January, nobody ever saw it again.

We spent about an hour with the lapwing that overcast morning. We had other activities planned and I had a final exam to give. Whether the lapwing arrived intentionally, assisted, or simply lost its bearings, I'm grateful for its presence so coincidentally close to where we happened to be. It sparked wonder in an austere place, demonstrated poise, and lent me a new, more useful metaphor. It lent me inspiration too.

As winter bore down, fortified by whatever worms and insects it found, I hope the lapwing headed home. I hope it locked on a favorable course and gave everything it had. With equal determination, I hope we follow suit.

Philopatry

*The tendency of an animal
to remain in or return to
the area of its birth*

I'm lucky. I have a place I always want to return. It's a red, listing, clapboard cottage on a placid lake—a pond really—that an Olympic swimmer could cross in minutes. I dogpaddle across in thirty. Each summer of my childhood, my family piled our belongings into a derelict trailer, lashed an oil-stained, chewed up tarp across the top, and fled the flatlands of central New York for the undulating hill country of northeastern Pennsylvania. The cottage, passed down the family line, was a winning ticket for a nature lover. Faucet water came straight from the lake which meant—gloriously—showers were moot. The cottage didn't even have one. Drinking water came from a well, where we carefully avoided scooping up salamanders and frogs that shared it. "Best water there is!" my dad boasted. "The only water there is," my mother retorted, hauling our clothes off for an onerous day at the laundromat.

The living room sported a toaster-sized, grainy TV with spindly rabbit ears as tall as I was. The rabbit ears were critical; without endlessly adjusting them, Jeopardy clues were unreadable. The only other screens in our lives were the partially shredded ones on the creaky porch doors. Shoe-sized holes, where we'd lazily kicked the doors open, adorned the bottom of each screen, convenient for the rodents we subletted from. The doors were a Narnian wardrobe. Through them, I exchanged one world for another, one of dust and mothballs for sylvan glades and verdant ferneries.

On the edge of a glade, in a blackberry tangle, I imprinted on a yellow yarmulke. The donner of the yarmulke peered down from his saggy powerline perch at my archaic binoculars supported by twiggy legs, knobby knees and sapling frame. A horseshoe moustache ran down his face and bumped into brown suspenders that held up, well, nothing: His belly was spotless, gleaming white. Unimpressed with my frame, the bird tilted his yarmulke back and sang, flicking his wings for effect. When I lowered the binoculars, red rings encircled my eyes from mashing the eyecups against my sockets. I went through my mental flashcards: Robin, no. Cardinal, no. Goldfinch, no. Nuthatch, sparrow, blue jay. No, no, no. That covered the birds I knew. What was this exquisite creature that looked to have been hand painted by Michelangelo? The sylvan sprite bowed, sang once more, and disappeared into a curtain of green.

Later that evening, I squeezed my twelve-year-old limbs between my two older siblings on our musty, mouse-colored couch as Alex Trebek read the Final Jeopardy question. While my siblings puzzled over which island nation featured the two main religions of Greek Orthodox Christianity and Islam, I leafed through the yellowed pages of a Golden Guide, a pocket-sized field guide as weathered as the cottage it nested in. The simple title—*Birds*—belied the intricate designs of the organisms within.

Halfway through, spanning three pages, was a group of nine diminutive, finely marked birds, half sporting a saffron base coat. Four had weird names: ovenbird, yellowthroat, redstart, waterthrush, while the rest all shared "warbler" appellation. I ran my finger over each one, recalling the field marks I'd seen on my powerline bird: white belly, brown suspenders, black moustache, yellow yarmulke … nothing. No bird matched it.

The studio audience clapped for the winner while I, frustrated, snapped the book shut. Wait, a subtitle: *A Guide to the Most Famil-*

iar American Birds. Oh. Duh. Perhaps what I'd seen was unfamiliar, too unfamiliar for the Golden Guide to include. I flipped back to the warblers and read the short paragraph that prefaced the nine birds. One sentence stood out: "…An experienced watcher may see as many as twenty-five kinds of warblers on a warm May day if he searches enough."

Twenty-five? In one day? Yeah, right. I paged through them again. If these were the most familiar American birds, why didn't I recognize them? I had spent half my life outside, scaling turn-of-the-century rock walls and squishing through skunk cabbage. What did this book know that I didn't? Was I in the wrong place? Was I not looking hard enough? If the bird I found was indeed a warbler, could I, too, find twenty-five in a single day?

That day under the powerline changed everything. It was act one, the magical time you don't fully appreciate until its gone. A time when curiosity drove my steps and my judgment was unmarred by adolescence. Hormonal urges were blissfully dormant, responsibilities were minimal, and my imagination was a tinderbox. The Golden Guide and that winsome little bird, which a thicker field guide in the local library revealed to be a Chestnut-sided Warbler, ignited it. All these years later, the fire burns on.

I've seen incredible birds since. Andean condor, Somali ostrich, wandering albatross, Galápagos penguin. Yet none hold a candle to that chestnut-sided warbler. The bird consumed me, transporting me to loftier, more intricate world. I hadn't searched. The chestnut-sided warbler—*Setophaga pennsylvanica*—had been there all along. Under that powerline, I had developed eyes to see it.

Magical moments don't last forever. All too quickly I lurched into typical teenage awkwardness. Summer camps, construction jobs, a diploma, a driver's license, and college. My interests widened. Distractions and responsibilities increased. But the chestnut-sided warbler never stopped singing from the corner of my crowded life. Hearing it, I sniffed out a short-term job in Belize, working for an incipient—and now defunct—nongovernmental organization that sought to preserve rainforest through the promotion of research, development, and eco-tourism. Daily I cleared trails, sifted through moldy reams of data, and drove teams of American medical doctors around. At night, I lassoed geckos with dental floss and fed them to the tarantulas that lived in the dirt outside my dank hut. Mornings, with the rainforest enveloped in a shroud of mist, I wandered after birds.

On one meander, a cinnamon-colored royal flycatcher streaked across the narrow trail. In Pennsylvania, I would have followed it. Not here. The jungle was too thick, the trail too easy to lose track of. Though early, humidity was high. Perspiration trickled down my temples. My clothes, worn for several days straight, matched the forest's color and clamminess. A day earlier, while raking debris, I'd noticed a pellucid, waist-deep pool adjoining the trail. With other researchers not yet awake, the time was ripe for a bath. I was ripe for a bath.

Reaching the pool, I stripped down to boxers and waded in. Ahh. As refreshing as advertised. Crayon-sized fish with tiger stripes nibbled my toes as I eased in. Soon, only my eyes and nose pierced the glassy surface. Sunlight stabbed the canopy and lit up the pool with a dozen saucer-sized spotlights. The amoeboid pool engulfed me in its watery womb. Above offered a wide-angle window of the tangled, liana-strewn canopy. A lone vine, no thicker than a garden hose, dangled parabolically over the pool, its nadir three feet from my face. I closed my eyes and exhaled. Nirvana.

Too often in the tropics, skinny vines turn out to be snakes. Not this vine. It was a perch, and the world's most convenient perch at that. However long later, I opened my eyes to the lemony underside of a warbler affixed to the bottom of the U-shaped vine, just above my nose. A black hood draped over the bird's body. The face was yellow, the inverse of a Zorro mask. Warblers are spastic, flit-happy birds. Their turbo-charged, ten-gram bodies bounce around the boughs like ping pong balls. Not this warbler. It sat contentedly, foregoing the opportunity to glean, preen, or sing. Thankfully, it didn't defecate. We just were. Two fellow travelers sharing a small, sacred moment. The bird had traveled the same path I had. Unlike other birds I'd seen in Belize—manakins, motmots, oropendolas—I knew this one. Truly knew it. A fellow northeasterner, a bird that migrated every spring to North America, to find a mate, weave a small nest into the fork of a young sugar maple, and raise a family. Perhaps this bird traveled the same path I had. Perhaps it shared my little Pennsylvanian woodlot. Not long after spying the chestnut-sided warbler, I found this one too—the hooded warbler.

"Beauty is not about perception, is not in the eye of the beholder," Barry Lopez writes, "but is the outcome of the artist's relationship with the world." I was a sojourner, not an artist. But since my warbler-enriched childhood, my relationship with the world had deepened. I began to know them, what they did, and where they belonged—in the hills of eastern Pennsylvania to breed, and here in the Central American tropics to refortify. The hooded warbler's place spanned two continents. Spring and summer were frenzied. Here, now, it exhaled. The warbler was at peace.

Lopez has words for these moments. They are "the first step in the neophyte's discovery of the larger world outside the self, the landscape in which wisdom itself abides." While the chestnut-sided warbler invited me in, the hooded warbler revealed joy that comes through knowing a piece of it. A lemony-feathered piece, weighing two nickels, that flew 3,200 miles to perch above my nose.

Decades later these warblers perch in my soul. While so many other moments have leaked away, these are etched like lithographs. "People are made of stories," Ted Chiang writes in *Exhalation*. "Our memories are not the impartial accumulation of every second we've lived. They're the narrative that we have assembled out of selective moments." Chiang's right. And with each passing year, I lean ever deeper into these moments, these warblers. They have become my narrative.

It's probably why I couldn't help myself when my dad recently called to inform me of his notion to sell the lake cottage. I raised a stink.

Everything he said made sense. He and my mom are older. They live in Florida. They haven't used the cottage in years. Nobody, barring rodent nation, has. Nature, abhorring a vacuum, laid siege. Fungi now sprout from the porch steps. Piano-heavy piles of leaves threaten the roof. Fallen branches crisscross the yard. One dock floated away. The other sunk.

Passersby abhor a vacuum too. Like the fungi, they see possibility and renewal. Though the century-old cottage has never been listed, they've made offers on the property. Though unstated, their intentions are clear: the cottage will be deep-sixed, the reign of rodent entropy will cease. In its stead will rise a gleaming, ahistorical palace.

Philopatry hasn't ruled my family as it has others. My siblings and I have all dispersed, jobs and spouses luring each of us states—and even countries—apart. Two gave the green light to sell. The other two, my sister and I, not so much. Neither of us have the time or resources to rehabilitate the cottage. My sister has a lake cottage of her own. I travel a lot. Come June, my three acres grows like a Belizean jungle. I hack away trying to keep nature at bay, to keep my own little house upright.

The cottage passersby are surely correct. The cottage should be interred. We should move on; I should move on. As much as I love the rough-hewn walls and exposed beams, it isn't the thoughts of a teardown that rankle me. My tailspin is deeper than nostalgia. "Grief," I read once, "is just the continuation of whatever the relationship was that you had."

I bear warbler grief. Corny, yes. But the thought of those warblers flitting about my old haunts, building nests, and raising families sustains me. Though I'm not there, they are, maintaining the storied trails of my childhood. Together we shared a stage during my life's most formative time. Inability to relive these moments—the stark ephemerality of them—heightens their importance. Grief and gratitude are inseparable.

I am thankful. For the chestnut-sided warbler revealing what I didn't know and the hooded warbler revealing what I did. I am thankful for the roles they played and their crisp, colorful costumes. On one, a black hood over a yellow body. The other white with brown suspenders, a black moustache, and that dashing yellow yarmulke. A yarmulke that became a golden guide.

Grief, gratitude and a niggling question: How does this act end?

Ownership

The act, state, or right of possessing something

American Turkey

A lake cottage isn't the only property passed down my familial line. My grandfather, a doctor, investor, and hunter, passed a mountainside along as well. The fifty-seven-acre mountainside, lacking a level place for a game of chess, is on a vertiginous slope in eastern Tennessee. Last time I checked, it still belongs to my parents; they're paying taxes on it at least. Like the cottage, offers trickle in. From hunters, developers, and locals hoping to buffer their backyard from hunters and developers. So far, my parents have refrained. Here's what I know: Mountainsides are finite. Demand isn't. The clock is ticking. That's why I recently set off to investigate. I needed to see my side of the mountain before it disappeared.

My plan contained one nontrivial wrinkle: Nobody knew where the mountainside was. Nobody, that is, except the sole remaining connection to my grandfather, an old turkey hunter named Larry.

Larry, it turned out, was more bird than human. I met him at an official Elizabethton, Tennessee, workplace: Waffle House. Larry was a seventy-something-year-old retired pharmacist much younger than my grandpa when they hunted together. "Let's have us some eggs 'n grits," Larry suggested, a twinkle in his unblinking brown eyes. A frowning waitress walked up and plunked two ceramic mugs on the table. Three-inch-high bangs threatened to crash onto her forehead; the 1980s were obviously too good to leave behind. "This here's a grandson of doc," Larry said, pointing to me with his chin.

"The usual?" she asked, not bothering to feign interest in my genealogical tree. She popped her gum as she poured light brown water into our mugs.

"Yes'm," Larry said, handing her the unnecessary menus from our table. The waitress scurried off as I cradled my cup, steam rising off the top.

"Do you still hunt?" I asked Larry, noticing a slight tremor as he sipped.

"Got seventeen birds this year."

"Seventeen?" I repeated, dumbfounded.

"Have you heard of the grand slam?" Figuring we weren't talking baseball or tennis, I shook my head.

"It's getting a turkey in every state, Florida to Maine, in a calendar year. To get a slam, you gotta keep drivin' north as the seasons open."

"You've done that?"

"Seventy times. Good for second place all time."

"Hold on. Seventy times you've driven from Florida to Maine bagging a turkey in each state?" Larry nodded.

"I've done a few royal slams, too."

"Royal slam?"

"Same as a grand except you gotta get a bird in Mexico, too."

"How many royal slams do you have?"

"Thirty-nine." I hadn't been to Mexico once, much less bagged a turkey there. Birding for Larry was entirely different. The waitress interrupted us with two steaming platters, and Larry held out his mug for a refill. "Thank you, ma'am." After a perfunctory prayer, Larry picked up his fork and pointed it at me. "Your granddad was really special to me." I looked away as his eyes turned misty.

"To me, too," I said. "That's partly why I'm here. My grandpa talked about you a lot." Larry looked out the window. He was clearly reminiscing. "Do you deer hunt, too?"

"Some. Gave it up mostly."

"Because you've gotten older?" Larry shook his head.

"Prefer bird huntin'. Also, I learned something about turkeys most folks don't know." I looked at him expectantly. "Learned I can call 'em in the fall, too."

That small comment explained how Larry's life unfolded better than anything else he said. Content to count flock sizes I saw to and from work, I had only dabbled in turkey hunting. Larry lived for it. Rather than fit a hobby around work, he fit his work—his life—around turkey hunting. Everybody knows that in northern climes, birds breed in the spring; hence why they can be lured. Spring is the time hen-focused toms lower their guard, when prurience leads them in range of a hunter. Turkeys are astoundingly wary; I rarely see them before they see me. Though most states have fall and spring turkey seasons, none of my hunting friends bother in the fall—it is too hard. Fall is for deer; spring is for turkeys. But none of my friends are like Larry. They don't talk turkey.

For much of the nineteenth and twentieth centuries, nobody talked turkey because there simply weren't any turkeys to talk to. We had hunted them all down. But, unlike the less fortunate passenger pigeons and heath hen, turkeys hung on, a few cagey, out-of-reach populations eluding postcolonial, market-driven avarice. This may be why, as Joe Hutto points out in *Illumination in the Flatwoods*, the wild turkey is the only bird in North America with "wild" as part of its common name. Not only does it distinguish the bird from the domesticated variety, as Hutto points out, "it also denotes the wild turkey's most conspicuous characteristic—that it is profoundly inconspicuous. Frequently," he concludes, "I encounter people who have never observed a wild turkey even though they live in an area where these birds are considered to be abundant."

Eggs and grits finished, I tailed Larry's Toyota Tundra across Elizabethton in my rental Corolla, barely able to keep up as he wove his way to the county clerk's office. The metal detector was the only thing that slowed him down. "Sir, you can't take that in," the security guard said, pointing to the five-inch-long jack knife Larry had dropped in a bin. "Nothin' personal." Born into a generation that stowed shotguns in school lockers for after school hunting, Larry stared at him confused.

I jumped into the generational stalemate. "I'll run it out to your truck for you," I said, grabbing the knife. Once the knife had been secured, we were led to a line of chairs in a sterile hallway. But when a woman with curly, slightly graying hair appeared, Larry's vitality returned.

"Well I'll be, you certainly look familiar. Hi Barbara!"

"Larry! How are you?" Barbara wasn't the person we'd come to find. But she had worked for Larry at some point and was eager to help us out.

"This isn't my domain, but let me see what I can find," she said, winking. Barbara disappeared into a room down the hallway and soon emerged with what we'd come for: tax maps demarcating fifty-seven acres of land on a flank of Walnut Mountain.

"Now listen," Larry said as we walked out into the sunshine. "I haven't been on Doc's land since I bagged a jake up there. Best I recall, whole thing's near vertical. Not sure there's a place fit for a picnic blanket. Don't think there's an access road neither. If you wanna see that land, you gotta walk," Larry said. "See this line?" He pointed to a portion of what looked to be a hand drawn map. "This is the river. Your land abuts that. But private property is backed up to that, so the only approach is from the other side." Larry paused and motioned to the horizon. "Untold miles of state land on the other side. I used to follow old logging roads. But they peter out soon enough. Never did know exactly where your gramp's land was. Just kinda figgered."

Rats. While the tax map was a lifeline, this land-finding mission was a fool's errand. Inaccessibility explained why the land remained in our familial line. Sloping, roadless, and bounded by a river, few had expressed interest until lately. But the land's marginality—that it had been deemed worthless by others—attracted me. Surely, this was wilderness as the 1964 statute saw it: "a place where the earth and its community of life are untrammeled by man." The possibility of stewarding such a place—of custodianship—excited me.

"Do you know the best way in?" I asked Larry as we paused by his truck.

"I know the only way in," he said, fixing me again with his no-nonsense stare. "An unmarked trail off a forest service road. Last time I was up there, some time back, the trail, if you'd call it that, was a sea of mountain laurel. Not sure if that little rental of yours'll make it up the mountain. Follow as far as you can. I'll point out the spot to start hikin'. You got a tent and gear, right?" I nodded.

One teeth-rattling hour later, I eased the muddy Corolla off the side of the heavily rutted road behind Larry's truck. "Been a druggie my whole life," Larry said, fishing around in the bed of his truck. "Opened Burgie Drugs, Elizabethton's first drug store." I chuckled. "Journey's not been without incident," Larry said, slipping a small black shoulder bag on. "Store's nearly been robbed three times, people desperate for meds and all." My eyes widened. "Nearly," he repeated, a gleam in his eye. "Got to the point that when a suspicious vehicle showed up, I'd head outside with my double barrel. The sight of it was enough for most. But I shot over the top of the store for good measure."

"You shot over the top of your store?"

"Sure did. Almost gave Barbara a heart attack every time. Would-be robbers had second thoughts." It dawned on me what was in Larry's shoulder bag.

"This here is Vanderpool Ridge," Larry said, pointing his thumb toward the forest. "You'll wanna stay on this ridge for as long as you can, long after the trail poops out."

"How long?" I asked, hungry for specifics.

"Can't remember," Larry said, "Big 'ole toms back there though."

"What do I do after the trail poops out?"

"If memory serves, sink into a drainage and climb back up. Cross that and you'll be standing on your land. But again, not sure where it starts without a land surveyor." I patted for my phone in my pocket. I had downloaded a map. But it was a bad phone with a worse battery. Only two hours of battery life remained. Stupidly, I had forgotten my extra battery pack. The undetailed tax map and these vague verbal directions were all I had.

"Follow me," Larry said. "I'll point you the way." Larry walked into the forest, ducking under witch hazel. "Grown in a fair bit since my last visit." Grown in? What "in" was there to grow into? It took a very active imagination to see a trail here. Some twisting and turning later, Larry turned to look at me. "This ain't trail mix and Gatorade," he said, tapping the strap of his shoulder bag.

"I guessed as much." Larry didn't smile.

"Out here, it's not critters you need to be concerned about. Only a fool doesn't carry." I gulped. Larry looked off into the forest, "We ain't pilgrims ya know."

Wrong. I was clearly a fool pilgrim, searching for a piece of unmarked mountainside with a photocopied tax map and half dead phone. Even so, I sensed my late grandpa would approve. Typical for middle children, I had often felt overlooked among my siblings. But never from my grandpa. As if he sensed my insecurity, he spent time with me—fishing trips, the zoo, out to eat. My well-being mattered and I loved him for it. Cancer had taken him during my sophomore year in college and other than a cherished landscape painting he'd given me before he died, I had few physical reminders. If this out-of-the-way piece of land mattered to my grandpa, it mattered to me.

When the mountain laurel closed in completely, Larry stopped. "Suppose you can manage from here," he said, sliding hands into his pockets. I wished Larry would take me all the way. But he'd gone way out of his way. "Larry, why'd you do all this for me?"

He met my eye.

"I loved Doc Knapp," he said. "And you're his grandson."

Ancestry matters. It mattered to Larry, as did turkeys and the land he hunted them on. It mattered even more to the Cherokee for whom

the forest through which I was hiking— Cherokee National Forest—
was named. The Cherokee were the "Aniyunwiya," the first people
who settled, between 800–1600 AD. If time allowed, I hoped to later
visit nearby Sycamore Shoals, where the Transylvania Land Company
notoriously attempted the largest private real estate transaction in the
history of the United States. For the equivalent sum of ten thousand
English pounds in goods and silver, the company's founder, Richard
Henderson, attempted to purchase twenty million acres from the Cherokee with the intention of making it America's fourteenth colony.

The Cherokee Council was divided. One, Dragging Canoe, vig-
orously protested the deal's lopsidedness. He warned that it would
pave the way for his people's extinction, a prophecy that fell on deaf
ears. Fortunately, a technicality voided the deal. According to the
Royal Proclamation of 1763, only the British—not a North Carolinian
like Henderson—could purchase land from the natives. The deal fell
through, and Henderson's heist went belly up.

But the land grab was off and running. The Cherokee referred
to this part of Eastern Tennessee as "Watauga," "the land beyond."
Hard to access but not beyond the reach of Euro-colonial settlers. The
Cherokee gave until they had nothing left to give. Finally, spurred on
by Dragging Canoe, they made a last-ditch effort to oust the settlers
and reclaim their fertile valley—a place less than an hour from where
I stood. The Cherokee siege dribbled out after two weeks. Not long
later, they were forced to leave the land beyond.

Like most appropriated lands that fell into private hands, it was
subdivided, sold, and resold. As a busy doctor who made house calls
in the mountains surrounding Elizabethton, my grandpa unwound
from the rigors of his profession with hunting and fishing trips. When
he retired and left Tennessee, he sold off us his more desirable hold-
ings—the accessible, level ones. Standing in that grove of mountain
laurel with a tax map in my hand, ownership suddenly struck me as
preposterous. An abstraction forced upon a finite, palpable good. Was
my relationship to public land different than my relationship to land I
owned? Does relationship have anything to do with ownership? Own-

ership is abstract, relationship isn't.

—

Larry left. His quips about the need to carry, the thick brush, and the darkening, late-afternoon clouds unnerved me. Surely, I was the only weirdo within miles. This was a simple coddiwomple, my travel purposeful, my destination vague. Nothing to be alarmed about. I had camped alone many times. Relax.

Rain felt imminent as the ground underfoot started to slope away. Was this the edge of Vanderpool Ridge? According to Larry, I had to sink into a drainage and climb up the other side. Was this the drainage he meant? Worried I wouldn't be able to retrace my steps on the return trip, I broke branches and fashioned them into crude arrows on the ground. Wobbly under my pack, I slipped it off and slid to the bottom where my boots sunk into muck. What did Larry consider a drainage? This felt more like a swamp. Did I still have farther to go? Heavy raindrops fell. It's gotta be just up there, I thought, squelching out of the mire and scrambling up the opposite slope. When I crested it, the land fell away again. More mountain laurel, more muck, and another hill to climb. I pulled out my map and rotated it, hoping a different angle would add perspective. It didn't.

Was I on standing on our land? Or was it over the next drainage? Either way, I'd need my pack. Looking around, I retraced my steps. Had I climbed up here? Or over there? Rain increased. I looked at my phone. It showed I had walked for over an hour but covered little ground. How could I get turned around so easily? Willing calm, I paced a wide circle. Nothing. I did another increasing my arc. Ah! Phew. There it was. Thrilled to reunite with my pack, a grim realization dawned: I might never set foot on my grandpa's land. Or maybe, of course, I already had.

Then again, what did it matter? Was state land any different than our land? Did it matter if I was one hill—or three—off course?

Maybe the night would reinspire me.

That night—with thunderclaps, lightning, heavy rain, and a loud thump into the side of my tent—most definitely did not. The thump, which indented the tent's nylon well over my supine body, unnerved me even more than Larry's warning. Had a limb fallen? Had a possum blundered into it? Was it the snout of a sniffing bear? The rain nixed plans to hang my food. I had stashed most of it in the crevice of a nearby tree, except for a package of six frosted donuts lying next to me. If a bear was nosing around and eating my food, the pattering rain drowned it out. Fitfully, the night passed.

At dawn, I cautiously crawled out. Misty tendrils threaded through the forest, pierced by a trill of a worm-eating warbler. The stashed food was untouched; whatever had thumped my tent hadn't been ursine. I turned on my phone: 14 percent. Enough for an exit. Not enough for further reconnoitering.

A turkey would have found my grandpa's fifty-seven acres by now. "Turkeys in general have this misplaced reputation for stupidity," Joe Hutto writes. "They have a perfect memory of what the entire forest is supposed to look like. If any object is out of order, if a new limb has fallen out of a tree, they find that limb very disturbing."

I, on the other hand, had no idea what this forest should look like. My tax map didn't help. The map on my wet, dying phone showed relief, but included nothing about tree density or impassable muck. Unlike the Cherokee, my relationship with this mountainside was as thin as my rainfly. Worse, my initial motivation made me feel more like a latter-day Richard Henderson, justifying ownership as a means of deeper connection.

I craved certainty about this place. But I wasn't prepared. My timing was off. Even Larry's would-be pharmacy robbers had known when to cancel their plans. I rolled up my soggy tent and strapped it onto my pack. With a final look at the land beyond, I swung on my pack and headed back.

Territorial

*Relating to the ownership
of an area of land or sea.*

WHITE PELICAN

I have seen over two thousand different bird species. But how many do I know? How many, were I to see them again, could I say: ah yes, indigo bunting, I know that one?

At least a third of the birds I've seen, that perch upon my life list, I struggle to recall. I claim them but don't know them. On a mountain trail or in a reedbed, I spied them, took a hasty photo, and compared them to a picture in a field guide. Or, worse, let a local guide inform me what they were. Check. Such birds, seen on cross-continental forays with limited field time, fall away. I'm aging, my brain a sieve. But I can still learn. What I need now is context and repetition. If I sit with a bird and watch repeatedly, it flies into my memory. To learn new birds now, I must be patient.

But for a cherished few, one encounter is sufficient. When the bird and I—watcher and watched—partake in a moment of charged particularity, of mysterious alchemy. These few are more sacred than the rest.

Ella Sorensen braked so fast my body swung forward. "I'm not an activist." She looked at me, her piercing blue eyes locking mine.

"I'm territorial." I nodded, waving my hand to ward off the clouds of mosquitoes and midges filling the truck. Ella wasn't done. "I wield a machete. If they put one toe north of the Goggin drain, I'll chop it off." She wasn't smiling.

"They" were Salt Lake City developers. I'd been with Ella for less than an hour, but I didn't doubt her. She was a pit bull. Twice my age, half my height, and one hundred times more sincere. Decades earlier, she had set her teeth into a liminal piece of Great Salt Lake shoreline. She hadn't let go, willing the local Audubon chapter to turn four thousand acres into the Gillmor Sanctuary, a critical rest stop for migrating birds. While easier to locate than my parents' land in Tennessee, it was equally inaccessible and off limits to the public; I was here as a friend of a friend. A formidable series of padlocked gates barred entry. Ella shouted memorized combinations out the window as I fumbled to open each one. The sanctuary was for the birds. But all around it, titanic Amazon warehouses were sprouting up as developers championed an inland port.

"Here's where I see my sage thrashers," Ella said, gesturing out her window with her half-eaten Danish. Gooey crumbs, which she failed to see, flew about the cab like shrapnel. "Wanna chase them?" she asked, sapphire eyes twinkling. Butcher antagonists one minute, chase thrashers the next. I liked this woman.

Early morning sun ignited the crimson pickleweed carpeting the salt flat. Luminescent puddles pockmarked the fetching mosaic. "I was born over there," Ella said, pointing to a hazy blue hill on the horizon. "Born and raised in Utah. Dad was an Aztec buff." Personal and natural history spilled out as we walked. While I jotted down the name of a plant, she recited—quite loudly—two full-length poems by Nezahualcoyotl. Unless the local thrashers were hearing impaired, we weren't about to sneak up on any. I didn't care. Ella was a bottomless well of Utah knowledge. Her bird-land-water devotion—and charisma—was intoxicating. A shower of Danish spray was a small price to pay for her presence. Ella made territoriality feel virtuous.

"People have compared me to Rachel Carson, Georgia O'Keefe,

and even a burrowing owl," Ella said. "I love those owls, but I am unique. I know who I am and the whole world be damned." I didn't see the owl comparison, but the other two, with maybe a touch of Richard Simmons, seemed apt. "You see how Salt Lake City is mushrooming? The inland port is just the tip of the iceberg. Everybody wants this land. But I want it just as badly as they do. Only difference is, I want it for the birds." Ella paused and ran leathery fingers over an iodine plant. "Environmentalists can protest all they want. Some of them see me as a sellout. But if we want to protect this place, we have to work with everybody. Isn't this sand verbena delightful?" I nodded, scribbling furiously in my notebook. I hadn't anticipated words of compromise or her avalanche of non sequiturs.

"I brought the head Mormon bishop out here," Ella said, sidestepping a clump of tumbleweed. "I showed him the birds, told him why they matter. And you know what? He trusted me. Not long after that, he made a huge donation to the sanctuary. Without that money, we'd be walking in a warehouse right here." I looked around trying to picture the pickleweed and sand verbena squashed beneath a windowless building while forklifts scuttled about instead of thrashers. "Then, a senate dude and a house dude invited me out for dinner."

"Dinner? Why?"

"To buy me off. Scumbags, both of them. But I went. And you know what?" Ella stopped and looked at me, much the way Larry had on Walnut Mountain. "They liked me. As did the duck club dudes later on."

I understood how Ella won people over. She was unapologetically herself, hiding nothing and refusing to hide behind anything. She was a potty-mouthed, guileless straightshooter whose love of birds was equaled only by her love of these featureless salt flats. Holding my eyes prisoner, Ella then said something I'll never forget. "I think we might be kindred spirits."

"Really?" I asked, hopeful. She nodded.

"You get it."

I wasn't sure I did. But lest she cut my toes off, I wasn't about to contradict her.

For two decades, I had flitted about the world like a hummingbird among flowers. I was addicted to new places, new experiences, new birds. I was enamored with novelty; Ella by what she already knew: The Great Salt Lake now threatened by development. Each spring, she watched the dainty petals of golden current unfurl while the tips of avocet feathers lightly brushed the lake's mirrored surface. Now, the city was unfurling upon her place, warehouses brushing up against her priceless, austere ground. "What is behind your eyes," Gary Zukav writes, "holds more power than what is in front of them." I worried what lay behind my eyes, fearful it was deficient.

Ella held power behind hers. She also frequently lost her train of thought. "Oh look! Curly gumweed! I traced the line of Ella's finger to a small plant on the ground. "Can you believe this crisp air?" she said spinning around. "What were we talking about?"

"Weren't you telling me about the Aztecs?"

"Oh yes, the Aztecs. You see, Eli, the Aztecs were … pelicans!"

"The Aztecs were pelicans?" I arched an eyebrow, but Ella ignored my remark. With an outstretched arm, she traced a skein of incoming American white pelicans.

Ella watched them, and I watched her. A whirling dervish moments before, now she was a statue, as rooted as the Indian ricegrass underfoot. Flutelike notes of a meadowlark floated upon the breeze. Over the lake, the pelicans evaporated into nothingness. Ella didn't move. Chin up, she inhaled deeply. Slowly, her arm lowered. Neither of us spoke. There was nothing to say.

A month later, back home in New York, the phone rang. I glanced at the clock: 10:23 p.m. Uh oh. My heart raced. Phone calls past nine are never good. Stoically, I answered. It was my brother Andrew. This time he wasn't calling about a bird. His grave tone confirmed my suspicion. "Dad's had a cardiac arrest."

The next few days were a predictable blur. I cried, hugged my wife and kids, and flew to Florida. My dad survived. Within a few minutes of his cardiac arrest, an angelic first responder administered CPR and whisked him into the ICU, where he was now unresponsive and breathing through a ventilator. Andrew, my mother, and I sat bedside as nurses filed in and out, checked vitals, and adjusted equipment. We talked, paced, reminded each other to eat, and asked every nurse and doctor the same question: "Will he be okay?"

The doctor didn't know. The nurses' answers varied. One told us to hold onto hope, another to prepare for anything. A third, right before telling us we had to leave for the night, said unequivocally: "Nobody comes back from these." It was a soberminded quip; the recovery statistics for out-of-hospital cardiac arrests were bleak, hovering around 10 percent. Fewer still return to their former, multifunctional lives. I had to leave Florida two days later.

Just in case, I told my dad goodbye.

Dad has long flouted conventionality, so my goodbye proved unnecessary. Long recovery odds were just another surmountable hurdle. For the next two months, we all took shifts going back and forth to Florida, rearranging work schedules, ferrying my mother around, and updating the family chatline. Improvement came little by little—appetite, speech, recognition, mobility, recalcitrance—then all at once. When he demanded coffee instead of water, we knew it was really him. To our joy and amazement, he was soon discharged.

At the end of my second visit, I walked outside the recovery unit where my dad was being monitored. On the horizon, in the early morning light, two large dark birds appeared over a string of cream-colored apartment buildings. Struck by their beauty, I fumbled for my camera. Then I stopped, hand halfway into my shoulder bag. I had seen, documented, and tallied enough. Stacks of bird albums and trip lists in my cluttered office testified to that. I raised my arm skyward.

It was America's other pelican, the rown pelican, once endangered and now fully recovered. Like my dad, this pelican had needed help, a place to rest and recover. Sanctuary. I watched the pair tilt on the wind, arc south, and dissolve into nothingness. A sacred moment.

Slowly, my arm lowered. Chin up, inhaling deeply, I watched the sky long after the pelicans had disappeared.

Nomenclature

*The devising or choosing of
names for things, especially
in science or other discipline*

RED-TAILED HAWK

K nowing a bird usually happens slowly. Knowing a place even more so. If the salt flats of Utah are a cleanly swept floor, then my place—the lumpy hills of western New York—resembles a messy room with a green blanket tossed overtop. Unlike the sublime Wasatch Range that rims Great Salt Lake, this fine, fertile country doesn't adorn inspirational wall calendars. New York City rises six hours east. Having ducked developers' attention, it's peaceful, overlooked, and typical rural America: Scrubby, second-growth woodlots, weed-choked pastures, and, two miles out of any town, lonesome houses floating amid oceans of corn.

It's glacial land. Fifteen thousand years ago, mile-high ice bulldozed and scraped everything in its way. South, north, south, north—the glaciers advanced and retreated, sometimes stagnating, dumping willy-nilly. Sand here, gravel there, and in the spring, squishy clay eager to suck off a loosely tied shoe. America boasts many grander, postcard-worthy places, with higher peaks, taller trees, and longer sightlines. But like a favorite sweater, this little overlooked cranny— saggy, soggy, overlooked—fits. "Well Eli," an old friend recently mused, "you gotta be somewhere." He's right. I'm somewhere.

And now is the time to know my somewhere as Ella knows hers, to define my relationship with this land, to become more than friends.

Since relationships are born of time together, I head out my door, time in one hand, coffee thermos in the other, the latter to ensure I won't let too much blood enter my caffeine stream. A book rounds out my accessories.

Freed from classes, I pick my way through knee-high grass in route to the forest's inviting June coolness. I stumble upon a fawn, follow a fritillary, and fruitlessly estimate the number of porcupine pellets in a pyramidal pile at the base of an old, fissured hemlock. Hoping to spy an owl, I investigate blue jay alarm calls. Instead of an owl, the barred tail of a Cooper's hawk disappears into a tangle of honeysuckle. As ornithologists know, birds are predictable only to a point.

An hour in, I grow tired of constant intrusion. I desire sublimation, to give up my loud body and blend in, to be among the wildlings rather than apart. I'm tired of watching the white semaphores of nervous deer wag away in bounding leaps. I want stillness and silence, for the deer to bumble into me, stamp their feet, and think: "How long have *you* been here?"

It's time to sit. Tree stumps long sufficed. Now, in midlife, I opt for collapsible camp chairs. I've stashed them about the forest on prior rambles, in hollow logs, stream undercuts, near convenient sites with decent sightlines. A student, whose name I often forgot, recently gave me a mug: "If you were a bird, I'd remember your name." (In my defense, it was the pandemic; all thirty-five students were masked. Attendance was spotty.) But the truth is undeniable: Bird taxonomies hang in my mind better than student names. Stashed chairs, however, are equally seared on my hippocampus. Their presence beckons me. I'll smile from the grave when a future hiker finds a mildewy camp chair sticking out of an old fox den.

Professors, the stereotype goes, are absentminded. I lean into this, cultivating it with unanswered emails and a piece of tape over the infernal blinking red light on my office phone that reminds me my voicemail memory is full. Previous head-in-the-clouds academics set the bar low; I've cleared it with ease. My students don't expect prompt email responses, so they are gleeful when I come through. "Wow, Professor Knapp, I didn't think you'd *actually* write back." I didn't think I would either. Sometimes I feel bad. Protestant guilt is hard to shake entirely.

The metaphor really is apt: My head truly is in the clouds. It's in the fields and forests, too. I don't have much time to sit inside these cathedrals and join the worshipful paeans. Dulled and distracted by screen scrolling, I fear a shortage of spectators at nature's great show. Lookouts need lookouts. Sitting here, it seems, is the least I can do.

This ramble has led to a favorite lookout. It sits atop a heavily eroded bluff that claims a few more hemlocks every spring. It's usually the last stop on the line, the endpoint of my forays. I arrive, flick a few slugs off the chair, and settle in. The possibility that I'll be the bluff's next victim injects drama; life on the edge for a guy who's scared of needles, motorcycles, and cubicles.

Here is the perfect counterbalance to a semester of arguing viewpoints, a simple view from a point. I gravitate to it evermore, a place to contemplate my existence, to ensure I'm taking stock of what truly matters—blooming, growing, withering—the cycles of significance. The view from this bluff is spectacular in its ordinariness: a distant barn and silo, a lightly traveled road, and, fifty yards below, a mercurial milky waterway. A naturalist friend once told me that you hop across a creek, wade across a stream, and swim across a river. If so, this is a stream. But up here, feeling like a potentate, I issue an edict: creek. Not crick, mind you. I live too far north and have too many teeth, to call it that.

An old road loosely parallels the creek's contours. Since it mostly leads to tucked away homes, nobody is in a hurry. Matchbox-sized pick-ups creep along, horns for greeting rather than gridlock. A great blue heron flies over the creek, flapping languidly, silent and purposeful, as if pulled by a string. I watch it disappear to the east. Peace like a heron.

"Some poor, phoneless fool is probably sitting next to a waterfall," Duncan Trussell writes, "totally unaware of how angry and scared he's supposed to be." Why isn't every bluff, I wonder, peppered with poor, phoneless fools in collapsible camp chairs?

It's early. A school bus crawls by. Glad those days are over, I think, grinning into my coffee. Minutes pass. Maybe an hour. My book remains upside-down, a coaster for the cap of my thermos. If I run out of thoughts, it's there, ideas to teleport me other places, other worlds. This morning, here is enough. "Nature is a place 'out there,'" Ellen Meloy writes in *Eating Stone*, "the not-home place, much as history is 'back then,' the not-us time. We attend both by random visits." Meloy's right. I want to make nature here, make my visits less random. Make it my at-home place.

A red eft crawls beneath the shaded parasol of a mayapple leaf, his flexible toes curling around whatever they touch like octopus tentacles. The plaintive song of a veery twists up around me like helices. A pencil-thin beech rises above a light green fern fiddlehead. One of last year's skeletal leaves hangs from it like a neglected Christmas ornament, gossamer veins bathed in sunlight.

So much to miss had I stayed home tethered to Wi-Fi. There, marching orders, requests, and queries arrive through technology I've forgotten how I lived without. Gutters need cleaning, decks need staining, outbuildings need to be purged and de-moused.

Tasks are blissfully out-of-mind here; my to-do list short and doable: Breathe. Watch. Be.

An hour folds into two. A red-tailed hawk soars into view. Seconds later it draws parallel, eye level. Something squirms in its talons. The hapless creature, on the ride of its life, flails. Rabbit? Squirrel? Mink? Now a stone's throw away, the all-seeing hawk startles at the sight of a gawking, sedentary ape, and its talons splay reflexively. The creature falls headlong into the roiling creek below. I leap up, but raspberry tangles clutter my view of the impact. The hawk flies on. Breakfast gone it'll have to catch something new for brunch.

I call my bluff. Formerly nameless it is now christened: Hawk Drop Creek. A memory tied to a place, written by attentiveness. Hawk Drop Creek isn't alone. Other parts of my local landscape have assumed nomenclature, known only to me. Iron Seep is a rusty ooze that stains my boots orange if my jump falls short. Woodpecker Way is an old stand of half dead basswoods, where I spent a pleasant afternoon watching red-bellied woodpeckers feed a begging brood. Timberdoodle Trace is a scruffy, overgrown field a male woodcock strutted through two summers ago. The names are mine but the places name themselves, springing up at once, like mushrooms after a hard September rain. They dissolve away when I move on, meaningless to everybody but me. But for now, they're important, little symbols of attachment that lend meaning to an overlooked landscape.

Until now, I've shared my names with no one, certainly not the conventional farmer who owns the vast acreage abutting Hawk Drop Creek. Two decades in, I've yet to meet him. The people that work his untold acres are hired hands, none of them tied to the place as I am. When one rumbles by in a towering combine, I ease behind a hedgerow knowing my presence will go unnoticed. Uncharitably, I picture this farmer as Oz. Yet rather than behind a curtain, I see him dwarfed by computer screens under incandescent lights, phone in one hand, computer mouse in the other.

I like to think that my view on his bluff is more expansive, my lifestyle more virtuous. Reality says otherwise. We're tethered together, our truths intertwined. My consumption habits fuel the farming practices around me; the farmer, his workers, and I all locked in the same industrial food complex. Complicity gnaws at me. "Conquerors," Wes Jackson writes, "are seldom interested in a thoroughgoing discovery of where they are." I head outside, walk the land and name the creeks to ameliorate my guilt, to prove Jackson wrong.

I've met several of the hired hands. Affable but distant, they are willing to chat a minute but eager to move on to the next set of fields a township or two away. Attachment here is thin; it's where work is, little more. Two times a year, their quarter-ton pickups line my dead-end road, as they work the fields in large-wheeled combines wider than my house. The engines rumble well past nightfall as high-powered headlights illuminate the corn rows like an airstrip.

Owned but unknown, these fields were acquired for return on investment. In the fall, after the corn has been sheared, hunters lease the fields in hopes that lovestruck ten-pointers wander through. I steer well clear during rifle season, eager to remain upright and keep my body unperforated. In winter, if the snow is right, I strap on skis, follow coyote tracks, and exhale with the sighing land. Respite is short. Come spring, the combine parade will return to till, plant, and spray.

We're accustomed to these phases. But some years, when the noxious glyphosate lingers in the air and our windows won't close any tighter, we grouse with our neighbors and take action. We make phone calls, wring our powerless hands, and nervously Google symptoms of non-Hodgkin lymphoma. Next year, the farmer assures us, he won't spray. We roll our eyes and pray that two decades from now, we won't grow a third eye.

Our story isn't unique. Across America, complaints fall on deaf ears. The balance of power is weighted toward the industrialized farm. The web is complex. We The Consumers haven't figured out how to untangle ourselves, strands connect to political administrations, multinational companies, and the subsidized products we purchase. Every spring, all across America, biodiverse places get swept into vast, monocultural seas. Patented, bioengineered, and fungible, hegemonic corn marches on, row by row, exhausting the soil underfoot, ever more dependent on synthetic fertilizer. Nature abhors a vacuum, but any ecologist will tell you that it abhors a sterile monoculture more.

When the combines finish their final lap, I grab my thermos and book and head out. I skirt the tasseled infantry, wind around century-old rock piles, and step over rusty rolls of barbwire. I treasure the stony margins and the swampy gullies. Unfit for tillage, they are perfectly fit for me. The farmer, workers, and hunters ignore everything beyond the fields and deer stands. So I pay attention. I vow to know it for them, walking, watching, and naming. The farmer scales up. So I scale down. I peek under logs, probe in dens, and peer through my hand lens. A turkey feather here, an oak apple gall there, and my favorite gully dweller—a seven-trunked hickory. Every foray affirms an age-old ecological truth: There's no such thing as a vacant lot. Slow as I go, I miss much; I passed a cherry grove three times last summer before noticing a dropped deer antler. The antler was smooth. Absence of tooth marks assuaged my ego: Rodents hadn't noticed it either. Now, I tread Antler Ave more carefully.

Impositions are made upon this land, subtraction and extraction. I'd buy it if I could, give it a well-deserved break. For now, attention is all I can offer.

Surely, Hawk Drop Creek once went by another name. Two centuries earlier, Seneca feet padded out trails on the tired sod combines now crush. The Seneca people, members of the Iroquois Confederacy and keepers of the western door, hunted, fished, and farmed here. Arrowheads, mortars, and pestles pop up in each season's pass of the plow. They lived and they named, sonorous nomenclature largely scrubbed out and replaced with names with faraway roots: Belfast, Warsaw, Cuba. Other towns—Amity, Friendship, Freedom, Bliss—replaced Seneca names with high hopes of Euro-colonial idealism.

But nothing can replace the meaning behind Seneca names. Those that survived the cut make me smile. Cattaraugus, a neighboring county, means "foul-smelling banks," a translation yet to appear on a tourism brochure. Another adjacent town, Canaseraga, means "among the milkweeds." These old Seneca names, their fading translations relegated to out-of-print books and aging local historians, encourage my own naming efforts. "Their name is on your waters," historian Arch Merrill wrote, "Ye may not wash it out."

I don't plan to. They remind me that this land meant more to the Seneca than return on investment. Hawk Drop Creek flows into the Genesee, a Seneca name meaning "pleasant banks." If I stash my chair and walk several hours southwest, I enter Caneadea, "where the heavens rest upon the earth."

Nomenclature follows me home. With nowhere to go during the pandemic, we turned our attention to our home place, three little acres rimmed by a (hoppable) brook. "Fort Corona" emerged out of goldenrod stems and an old rail fence. Another ambitious fort, whose roof blew off in a gale, subsequently became "Fort Sadness." My office, "The Aerie," perches above our prosaically named "Nature Trail," lovingly demarcated by a sign painted by my daughter, Indigo. Scores of other names dot the yard. For these I leaned on science and our overtaxed label maker. Shiny strips of tin with multisyllabic Latin names, dangle from my yard's reachable flora. "A two-year-old can name more than thirty different plants and four-year-olds can recognize nearly one hundred," writes Carol Yoon of the Tzeltal Maya of Mexico, in her book *Naming Nature.* My children have a long way to go.

I harbor no such aspirations for my brood. Yes, I want my kids to go beyond "bush," "tree," and "flower." I want them to recognize that names presage meaning, attachment, and love. But times have changed. Their lives don't depend on the coltsfoot and Christmas fern growing in the ravine; they have other things on their minds—sleepovers, band, afterschool jobs—along with the usual mini-melodramas of youth. I don't wish my naming pathology on my worst enemy, and certainly not on them. But I do wish, long after the dust of adolescence settles, that they'll hunger to know their neighbors, human and nonhuman alike.

My watch isn't necessary to tell me it's time to go back. My thoughts have traveled further than I have, backward and forward, like a tide. Now they are in repose. I fold up my chair, tuck it back under the multiflora rose, and rise. Invisible as my contentment, it will remain as a lure to return, sniffed by a chipmunk, scaled by an eft.

I bid Hawk Drop Creek adieu, stroll down Antler Ave, cross Timberdoodle Trace, and went home. The air remains crisp, my breath condenses and disappears in the lambent rays, a small metaphor for my life, this special somewhere. I am a pilgrim at Hawk Drop Creek, hands empty yet full of grace. Unlike squirming prey, this gift is easy to hold onto.

Endemism

*The state of a species only
being found in a single
defined geographic location*

NORTHERN
MOCKINGBIRD

Mockingbirds are polarizing species. Their incessant desire to sing and imitate everything within earshot has made them famous or infamous, depending on how lightly one sleeps. They're symbolic, too, owing to Harper Lee's classic novel, representing everything from innocence to cleverness. For my dad, they symbolize annoyance. "Darn mocker!" he says as we sit on his lanai in Florida, where all the houses within three square miles boringly resemble each other.

I'm not so inundated with mockingbirds in western New York. That makes me a fan of *Mimus polyglottos*, the "many-tongued mimic." Up north, my patience is tried by the lyrically challenged eastern phoebe, whose scratchy, undeviating, two-note "song" makes me want to seal off my ears with duct tape. This makes the mockingbird, capable of singing over two hundred songs, a head-scratching maestro.

Adulation and scorn for these birds is everywhere. Scrolling public comments at the end of an article entitled "Mockingbirds Can Learn Hundreds of Songs, But There's a Limit," one person wrote: "Amazing birds. I now believe they are mocking boisterous toads here in North Carolina." Another: "I just adore the mockingbirds. This morning it imitated cardinal, grackle...and...believe it or not...DUCK!" Then,

more tempered: "Mockingbirds are charming indeed—until they dive-bomb you for inadvertently walking too close to their nests."
Mockingbirds have yet to divebomb me. But they have swooped into my life on three occasions, with three different people: a former president, an eminent biologist, and a neighborly farmer. The president and the biologist are long dead. The farmer is very much alive, though recently, he nearly wasn't. Since he's the least polarizing of the three and a good friend, he makes an amiable starting point.

Everybody needs a farmer in their life. Not an absentee owner several counties away; a farmer who lives in grease-stained overalls, a high-riding mesh hat, and looks off to the horizon while speaking. A person who welcomes drop-ins, can carry on a conversation as easily from under a tractor as atop one, and whose favorite form of weather is rain—steady, predictable rain.

Though my intermittent visits don't adequately reflect my admiration, I've long savored my friendship with Rodney. Time at his bucolic, mid-century farm is revitalizing, the antithesis of around-the-clock classes, committee meetings, and task forces. While I'm shuffling papers indoors, Rodney clambers atop a silo, positioning an augur. He notices everything, including birds. If his eye catches something unusual, I get a pithy email, to-the-point, and always graced with an invitation. "A new bird species for me, the northern mockingbird," he wrote last June. "What an array of songs. Everything from tree frog to red tail!"

Rodney's emails never ask for anything. I fired off a quick response, congratulating him on the bird and promising to come see it for myself. More quickly than usual, he wrote back. "Come anytime! It would be nice to confirm this mockingbird. It has been here four days and it's singing away now." The next line explained the speed of his reply: "We go to Rochester General tomorrow for the bone marrow biopsy. That will tell us the story."

The story was a diagnosis he'd received for AML leukemia. It had come on suddenly forcing him into bed. The prognosis didn't look good.

Our story, our friendship, started well before this, with another characteristic email.

"I read a piece of yours in *The New York State Conservationist*," Rodney wrote. "You should come by sometime. Got good land and birds you'd be interested in." An understatement, Rodney had great land and birds, nearly one thousand acres of upland woods, gently rolling hills, and fertile fields, bisected by the pleasant banks of the Genesee River. On the southern edge rose a steep-sided, hickory-covered knoll with a commanding view. The Seneca recognized the landform's significance and crafted a fort. Subsequent archaeological excavations discovered evidence of habitation, as had Rodney. On one of my visits, he pulled out boxes of arrowheads, mortars, and grinding stones that his plows had unearthed.

"Seems like a good birding spot," Rodney told me one day as he pounded out a bent axle. It was indeed. Since showing me "Fort Hill," I'd spent untold hours on the knoll, alone and with family. While I enjoyed wandering Rodney's land, watching him rehabilitate his arthritic farm equipment amid conversation was even better.

"Why did you decide to go organic?" I asked as the late afternoon sun edged toward a saggy roofline of one of his many barns.

"That one's easy," he said, unfolding a handkerchief and dabbing his brow. "Dual was the herbicide that changed my life. It's impregnated in plastic pitchers. After six months in a confined space with the pitchers, I could taste it in my mouth. One time I developed an awful headache and spent the next couple of hours salivating. The fumes alone made me nauseas and dizzy." Rodney toed a clod of dirt. "I couldn't do it anymore. Didn't feel right. That was the moment I went organic."

Dual wasn't the only dodgy chemical Rodney used in his attempts to keep his farm solvent. Unable to remember the chemicals he rattled off, he later sent me a list: AAtrex, Banvel/dicamba, Eptam/EPTC, Malathion, Prowl, Sonalan, Treflan, and 2,4-D—not to mention a slurry of adjuvants, stickers, solvents, and degreasers.

I'm a far cry from a chemist. But it doesn't take a scientist to realize you're better off not squirting these on your salad or snorting them in the barn. "Didn't you use Round Up?" I asked, all too acquainted with the chemical that forced us to close our windows each summer.

"Yes, glyphosate. Of course. Annually."

"But the Dual made you sickest?"

"Yes, and one other, Thimet, a granular insecticide. Whenever I was downwind after planting, I felt ill."

"So it was your health versus profit?" I asked.

"Oh, there was never profit, just varying degrees of debt. While those chemicals may increase your yields, none are free. Nor are the patented seeds. I've sold off a lot of land to make ends meet. Just one bad drought—or blight—away from bankruptcy." With resourceful devotion, Rodney defied the odds and hung on. Neighboring farmers sold out, kids grew up and moved away, and economies of scale consolidated small farms into massive ones.

Rodney's unique persistence stemmed from relationship. Like an enduring marriage, he understood how much his land could handle, its contours and tendencies, when to intervene and when to back off. Textured relationship allowed him to wean off the noxious brew. He repaired everything himself, survived a gruesome farm accident, and yet remained. Upright as a weathervane, Rodney is the rare exception, a lone point of resistance in the tidal wave of agricultural change.

During the dog days of summer, my family went on a presidential house tour in Virginia. My kids had been learning American history and the minivan we rented featured personal AC vents. In control of our own weather systems, I anticipated a squabble-free week. A built-in—and oft used—vacuum ensured we didn't ride in a growing compost bin.

Each of the four houses we toured, and the surrounding servant quarters, raised thorny issues about hierarchy, inequality, segregation, and slavery. A bit older, Ezra and Indigo peppered the thoughtful docents with questions. Five-year-old Willow fixated on originality. As our tour group trundled through Washington's Mount Vernon home, her hand shot up frequently. "Is this door original?"

"Yes."

"Is that candle original?"

"Sadly, no."

"Is that fruit original?" The docent frowned and shook his head. "Those are plastic reproductions."

"Is this window original?" The docent smiled.

"Yes." Each time she encountered originality, Willow approached as close as the docent allowed, inspecting each object carefully. Everything else—the reproductions—she ignored.

Willow's quest for originality continued at Jefferson's Monticello. With Rodney in mind, I was more taken with the mockingbirds. Their repetitive refrain easily penetrated the old walls and permeated the south wing. Discretely, I edged around the group and peered out the heavy-paned window. Other than an army of barn swallows swooping over the expansive north lawn, the raucous songster was hidden.

That changed in Jefferson's study. A mockingbird perched high up on a bookshelf, leering down at us. This time *my* hand shot up. "Did Jefferson carve that?" I asked, pointing.

"Afraid not," the guide replied. "It's here to represent Jefferson's fondness for mockingbirds. He loved them and daily fed them peanuts, sometimes from his mouth." Sensing my interest, he continued. "During Jefferson's time, Monticello didn't have mockingbirds, so the president purchased four of them. The first one arrived in 1793. We know this from a letter Thomas Mann Randolph wrote the president." The guide stopped. Another group was impatiently entering behind us. He couldn't humor me any longer and ushered us into the parlor. I lingered at the back, in the doorframe, unable to take my eyes off the mockingbird.

Like most songbirds, mockingbirds are philopatric: They return year after year to the same place. Their offspring follow suit. Lots had changed at Monticello since Jefferson's time. Trees had grown. Buildings had fallen into disrepair and been replaced. Countless furnishings had been whisked away where they could be better preserved. America had changed, too: A revolution, emancipation, world wars. Like the presidents, the nation had a checkered past. Constant change—adaptation in the face of changing ideals—one immutable attribute.

Bad timing. Jefferson was in Philadelphia when the first of his mockingbirds arrived in Monticello. Upon receiving Mann's letter, he immediately wrote back:

> I sincerely congratulate you on the arrival of the Mocking bird. Learn all the children to venerate it as a superior being in the form of a bird, or as a being which will haunt them if any harm is done to itself or its eggs.

Staring up at the carving, I puzzled over Jefferson's affection for this species. Was it just another of his mysterious quiddities? Or was it something deeper, a point of attachment for a man pulled in too many directions? As the winds of change swirled around his Virginian mountaintop, did mockingbirds drop him anchor?

When the HMS Beagle dropped anchor in the Galápagos Islands, mockingbirds met another person caught up in the buffeting winds of change: Charles Darwin. Change, in fact, obsessed him. During his five-week stopover on his round-the-world odyssey, he visited four of the thirteen recognized islands. Perhaps because he lacked peanuts, Darwin didn't pay lip service to mockingbirds the way Jefferson did, he shot and collected them, packing them up with plants, rocks, and other biological specimens.

Back in England, Darwin unpacked and arranged his reams of observations. Sadly, his mockingbird collection wasn't comforting. He had carefully labeled his plants, not so his birds. Leaning over the specimens in his study, differences in plumage were clear, his oversight clearer. "It never occurred to me," he wrote, "that the productions of islands only a few miles apart, and placed under the same physical conditions, would be dissimilar."

Before reaching Galápagos, Darwin recorded one mockingbird species in South America. Taxonomists today recognize three. Of the four Galápagos species, Darwin unwittingly collected three. Despite uncharacteristic sloppiness, he had a hunch the Galápagos formed an oceanic archipelago; that they had arisen from the sea rather than breaking off from another landmass. Labels or not, Darwin had zeroed in on endemism, a key concept in conservation biology.

Endemism refers to the state of being confined to one place. Conservationists rightly prioritize endemic species, limitation in space makes their survival more precarious than wide-ranging species. One event—disease, drought, or a highly competitive or predatory invasive species—can cause their extinction.

The world's mockingbirds, just like titmice, tanagers, and toucans, are variations on a theme. Their differences—bill lengths, wing patterns, overall sizes—are as measurable as their similarities. Darwin realized this. His Galápagos mockingbirds were different, but they clearly resembled those in South America. They must, he reasoned, share a common ancestor. He speculated: Perhaps a population of South American mockingbirds founded the Galápagos population. He speculated similarly, and more famously, with finches.

Darwin hadn't finished his deductive reasoning. If the Galápagos mockingbirds traced back to those in South America, perhaps all bird populations shared similar founding events? Perhaps common ancestry was just that, common? Perhaps it was traceable? Caution reined him in. His labeling lapse showed fallibility; the cart must remain behind the horse. He needed more—better labeled—data. Eventually, he acquired some. "This chain of inferences," the eminent biologist Ernst Mayr later wrote, "led Darwin to the ultimate conclusion that all organisms on Earth had common ancestors and that probably all life on Earth had started with a single origin of life."

Spurred on by the findings of Alfred Russell Wallace, another great biologist who arrived at a similar conclusion in Southeast Asia, Darwin finally published. Dominoes fell quickly but not decisively, and the fallout is well-known: ecclesiastical uproar, vitriol, name calling, monkey trials, attacks, defenses, more attacks, and latter-day entrenchment. Unsurprisingly, mockingbirds—those polarizing birds that never shut up—lit the fuse.

"It is the fate of every voyager," Darwin wrote upon his arrival back in England, "when he has just discovered what object in any place is more particularly worthy of his attention, to be hurried from it." I sympathize with and take solace in Darwin's sin of omission. Imperfection reveals a point of attachment for me, a lapse that makes him more relatable. It's also revealing. Amid all his seafaring, all his birding, and all his theorizing, Darwin was thinking about place.

Places shape species. That's what endemism is all about. But whom it applies to is less clear. The boundedness of populations is often blurry. Species don't always remain in one place. Willingly or not, they immigrate and emigrate. So like a newly hatched mockingbird, the concept remains fuzzy, begging for a firmer definition that doesn't seem to exist.

But the nest should be cleaned up on one count: An endemic species isn't necessarily indigenous. To be endemic, a critter doesn't need to have originated where it currently is. It could have arisen somewhere, strayed, and then—via climate change or habitat fragmentation—become marooned. Such a species is called, if you care, paleoendemic. Since you probably don't care, just remember this: Indigeneity is all about a place of origin; endemism where one is now. It's usually reserved for rarer species, or those in isolated places, like the Galápagos. That's why birders, like me, love endemics; you feel lucky to find one.

Darwin's mockingbirds are endemic. Not so the mockingbirds that annoy my dad, delighted Thomas Jefferson, and buoyed Rodney during his bout with leukemia. Biologists don't call them endemic at all. The many-tongued mimic is simply too widespread across North America to merit the term. Rather, they refer to *Mimus polyglottos*, our polarizing bird, as cosmopolitan.

Cosmopolitans are found the world over, endemics aren't. This makes a farmer like Rodney endemic, too. He has that rare trait my daughter Willow sought: Originality. Blown about by the winds of change, he adapted but remains. This makes him the best kind of rare bird. To find him, I toss my day planner aside and drive down the road.

Morphology

The form and structure of an
organism or any of its parts

Fox Sparrow

If you like neat and tidy birds, avoid the fox sparrow. The bird is messy. Nothing about it is foxy. Sadly, it is named for the other definition of foxy—"resembling or likened to a fox"—and only in color, not cunning. The bird is rusty-brown, rotund, and splotchy, disconcerting descriptors that might send us to a doctor. Darwin would have loved them—fox sparrows are poster birds for variability. They vary widely in appearance, migration habits, habitat choice, and song type. The poor birds can't make up their minds on anything.

To make sense of it all, birders lump the fox sparrow into morphs, which others call subspecies. As its name suggests, the "red morph" is just that, red. (Or, as I prefer, vulpine-colored.) This morph spans the northern part of the continent, bopping about the boreal forests of Canada. In the interior west resides a "slate-colored morph." This palette continues into the Sierra Nevada and Cascade Ranges, but there, birders fixate on its oversized bill and call it the "thick-billed morph." Yet another "sooty morph" is found along coastal Alaska and parts of British Columbia. True to their name, sooty morph fox sparrows appear to have flown out of chimneys, feathers covered in creosote.

Most sources recognize these four distinct types. Others, hair-splitters with too much time on their hands, claim eighteen fox sparrow subspecies. Like the Galápagos mockingbirds, fox sparrows are variations on a theme. Unlike those mockers, they're all considered one, a cosmopolitan species. No, they're not endemic. Don't bother memorizing this. Like much of taxonomy, tomorrow, all of it could change. I forgive you for not caring. Life is short. Why should you care about a common, streaky bird with four, or eighteen, different outfits? Because, beyond the soot, slate, and subspecies designations, the fox sparrow, *Passerella iliaca*, *is* worth caring about. If bill and plumage variation doesn't float your boat, know this: Morphological diversity is about something bigger: It's about how nature shapes us. How we're shaped by place.

It's also participatory. We make our place as we are shaped by it. For evolutionists who think about human origins, it's old news. Take hominid bipedalism, for example. A drying East African climate, some argue, spurred a population of knuckle-dragging apes to rise up on two legs. Rainforests gave way to savannas, and trees—especially fruit laden trees—became scattered. A bipedal gait, so the theory goes, conserved energy more effectively, enabling those upright apes to reach resources better.

Darwin, fascinated by tool use, went a step further (ahem). Such a transition, he thought, may have freed hands up for fashioning of weapons, usable in hunting and defense. Others point to the role predators may have played. Vigilance, a longer sightline, would improve the higher up one stood. Perhaps bipedalism allowed easier foraging, a longer reach? Or maybe, suggest the most salacious, bipedalism allowed other "members" to stand up, or out, to enhance phallic displays and mate acquisition? Since no sane scientist, thank heavens, is about to go test these hypotheses, we're left to speculate. Was it none, one, or some combination of these? We'll never know. The point is: Place—context—plays a role.

Though only skin deep, pigmentation provides a less speculative example of the shaping forces of the environment. The world over, pigmentation—skin tone—is correlated with the distribution of ultraviolet radiation, or UVR. Melanosomes in melanin help protect against

UVR. The protective shield is vital, too much UVR can damage DNA. So it's logical (and wonderful) that people who hail from equatorial regions, where potentially harmful UVR is present year-round, tend to be darker skinned. Conversely, when people migrated out of Africa, natural selection favored lighter skin. In northern latitudes, people faced too little exposure to sunlight, especially during long winters. There, darker skin made people more susceptible to vitamin D deficiency, which can lead to Rickets and a host of cancers.

A closet rebel, I've never been much into rules. But in ecology, I love them, especially as they pertain to observable phenomena. Allen's Rule, for example, explains why creatures in colder climates tend to have smaller appendages compared to their southernly relatives. It's simple: Colder places select for heat retention to ward off hypothermia. Warmer places, where overheating is possible, favor bodies better able to dissipate.

Gloger's Rule is another. This states that darker pigments are favored among populations in wetter climates with lighter ones more prevalent in drier places. As with pigmentation, Gloger's Rule is about protection, but against degrading bacteria, not UVR. Wetter places allow more harmful bacterial growth and contain more virulent strains of keratinolytic bacteria. Darker pigments keep these at bay.

For our messy fox sparrow friends, Gloger's Rule accounts for all those sooty morphs hanging about coastal Alaska. More inland, where it's drier, fox sparrows lighten up.

This jargon needs to lighten up too. Just a few more. In social science circles, shaping forces of the environment fall under a broad umbrella called environmental determinism. If the term sounds ominous, it's because it is. Too often misused, environmental determinism is the idea that the physical environment dictates the outcomes of a society. It removes human agency, giving primacy to climatic, ecological, and geographic factors. These factors, determinists argue, control cultural and societal development. Some have regrettably applied it to differences in human intelligence and accomplishment. It's been coopted, often racially charged and coupled with imperialism. Dark clouds indeed.

So there I sat, enamored with the way place shapes identities but leery of Machiavellian baggage. Fortunately the skies parted. On a verdant bluff overlooking the placid waters of Kachemak Bay, I wasn't alone. Above and to the right, a sooty cosmopolitan sang out.

The bluff wasn't mine. It belonged to a singer-homesteader-bird lover named Mairiis Kilcher, who went by "Mossy." Aptly named, Mossy had long clung to her bluff and fused with it. Today, she had invited a group of twenty of us from the Kachemak Bay Shorebird Festival. I'd spent the week speaking at the event, but in Mossy's company, I quickly realized I had little to say. Her Edenic, carefully tended acreage had a message all its own, Mossy its taciturn prophet. Her softly spoken sentences, the few that floated to the back of the stretched-out line where I was, meandered with the walk she led us on.

A compulsive lister and journal keeper, my record from the walk is uncharacteristically thin. Not for the lack of birds. Spring migration was at its peak, many passed us by. Yet I recorded only one, my entry as follows:

May 9, 2021
Seaside Farms
Fox sparrow

That's it. Three meager lines. No descriptions, musings, or quotes. Binoculars hung around my neck but this morning, I didn't reach for them. Five-year-old Willow's hand was snugly in mine. At the front, Mossy pointed to the left. A bird, teed up on the twig of a sapling, looked like an over-roasted marshmallow. Rotund and sooty, a fox sparrow. Mossy put a finger to her lips. Side conversations ceased. On cue, the sparrow tilted its head back and sang. A string of high-pitched staccato notes spilled out. Nothing flutelike or melodious—a toddler playing a penny whistle.

—

In 1977, Mossy recorded an album, *Northwind Calling*, a medley of stirring folk music centered on her love for Alaska. Like the sparrow, its greatness went largely unnoticed. But those who listened fell under its haunting spell. All twenty ballads are dedicated to Alaska, where Mossy arrived at age three, after her parents fled Switzerland and World War II with their eight children. Alaska's fierce storms and desolate winters terrified her, but she found refuge in the brave little birds that clung to the rugged coastline. Birds connected her to place.

In her teens, her parents ferried the family back to Switzerland. Mossy was miserable; she had imprinted on Kachemak's craggy mountains and moody sea. To cope, she taught herself to play the lute and composed odes to her beloved land.

Yearning for Alaska followed her everywhere. College, marriage, and a stint as a cattle rancher couldn't shake her desire to be home. For years, she roamed around Alaska as a nomad, living spartanly on a diet of crab meat. After living out of the back of her Triumph station wagon, she finally made it home, settling into her parents' old estate, Seaside Farms, the bluff where Willow and I watched her sooty, singing fox sparrow.

We listened to the fox sparrow for a long time. While others resumed conversation, Mossy stood silently, nodding at the bird. She smiled, her eyes shiny.

Later, I found out why. While several birds fly through her music, the fox sparrow has claimed one song all its own. The song takes the form of a question, its refrain as follows:

"He sings to the sea below
Will he be here tomorrow?
Will my children know
The song of the fox sparrow?"

I wonder the same for my children. Will they find significance in what is often overlooked? Will they yearn for home—and find it? One year after we returned from Alaska, Willow caught me staring out my bedroom window, a favorite all-too-frequent activity of mine. "Dad," she said, "do you know what I like about you?"

"Uh, no?" I replied, turning to look at her.

"You actually *watch* birds," she said, reaching for my hand.

Willow is right. I do watch birds. I'm captivated by their mind-bending variation, their responses to the environment, all their morphs. After that day on Mossy's bluff, I want to listen to them too.

Biomagnification

The process by which a compound increases its concentration in the tissues of organisms as it travels up the food chain

"Booby!" a lady shouted, spraying sandwich crumbs into the choppy sea. Thankfully, she pointed off the port side, not at a fellow boat passenger. I looked out. A whitish speck undulated with the waves. "We need that booby!" she yelled, her other arm waving binoculars at the skipper seated in the bridge.

Our tour boat, a bit shorter than a school bus, didn't yaw. Straight ahead, we crested and crashed over the Pacific's strengthening midday swells. The booby lady glared at the skipper, Debi Shearwater, who glowered back through wave-misted windows. Debi leaned into the crackly intercom and bellowed: "Safety comes first!" Click.

Unable to suppress my smile, I covered my mouth. So the rumors were true, Debi was a force to be reckoned with. I wanted to see birds. But this was really why I had come: To see my favorite movie, *The Big Year*, played out in real time. Like most birders, I savored the book and subsequent movie. Now cultishly adored, the story chronicled a competitive race between three obsessive birders to see as many US species as possible in a calendar year. Their race had pushed them all over the country and then out to sea, the only way to see the land loathing group of birds, called pelagics. To find pelagic birds, the three had boarded a boat—Debi's boat.

—

The Big Year enthralled me. Its basic elements—questing, competition, obsession, relationship, silliness—defined who I was. I seemed to be an amalgam of all three characters, warts and all. When I learned that one of the competitors, Greg Miller (played by Jack Black) was slated to speak at a birding festival in Maine, I zipped over with two vanloads of students in tow, to meet him. The day after his talk, I stood next to him on a boat, watching him watch birds. He scanned the horizon with alacrity and fist pumped his friends. His presence on countless pelagic trips didn't dampen his enthusiasm. "Check out those phalaropes!" He exclaimed as a loose flock of dainty, rednecked phalaropes whirled about our boat. Greg Miller, who ended his big year in second place with 715 species, didn't disappoint.

Debi Shearwater didn't either. An internet deep dive revealed that the movie producers had pegged her correctly. She did things her way. Unsatisfied with her surname—Millichap—she walked into a Santa Cruz superior court one day and changed it to Shearwater. Shearwater was sleek, hard to mispronounce, and the name of a group of birds that belonged to the sea, as she did. In the movie, her character balks at one of the birders (played by Luke Wilson) upset over wasting time watching whales when there were birds to find. What luck! On this boat, similar antics were afoot.

There was another reason I was on this boat. Shearwater was on the cusp of retirement. Worried I'd miss out, I booked the tour months in advance, hoping Linda wouldn't notice the dent in our checking account. After some university-related work down the coast in Santa Barbara, I had driven through the night, slapping myself to keep from drifting into oncoming semis on Highway 101. On an exit ramp for Monterey, I swung the car over on the shoulder. I needed to pee. I also needed to inspect a roadkill bobcat glowing red in my taillights. Bladder relieved and measurements taken, I pulled into a sleepy side street. Three a.m. That allowed two hours of glorious shuteye before I had to be at the boat launch. Could be worse. I set my watch alarm, reclined my seat, and conked out.

—

The plan worked. Around six o'clock in the morning, I joined twenty giddy others on the dock for Debi's opening safety talk. Nervous excitement mollified my churning stomach. Judging from the dorky outfits and array of optics dangling around necks, these were my people, used to sacrificing sleep and sanity for what they loved most: Birds. "There are some who have gone out hundreds of times," a guy remarked as we chugged out of the marina, "It's the only way to get 'em all." 'Get 'em all,' of course, referred to the rarest birds that most pelagic tours missed.

"How many trips have you taken?" I asked.

"This is my twenty-eighth. You never know what'll turn up."

A pony-tailed man in a camouflage durag butted in. "I'm gonna keep coming 'til I get Chatham's albatross," he said, fiddling with a setting on his camera. "Today may be the day." Restless optimism drove these two. But it didn't drive everybody.

"Are you here for a Chatham's albatross, too?" I asked a thirty-something woman beside me. The Svaroski binoculars around her neck could have paid off my mortgage.

"Oh no," she replied, steadying herself on a handrail. "I'm here for my father. Cancer got him last year. I can feel his approval when I'm on these trips. He loved these birds." I mingled with the others on board, picking up anecdotes, hoping to better understand myself.

"Risso's in the wake!" Debi announced over the intercom. Aboard long enough to learn the code, we lurched our way from the bow to the back, where Risso's dolphins were slicing through the waves. Squeezed in a mash of bodies and swinging optics, I cut through the main cabin where seaweed-colored passengers lined the benches. One stared vacantly at the floor while another breathed into a bag. In the corner, a curly-haired teen was scrolling. From an earlier conversation, I'd picked up that his dad had brought him for quality time together. Fat chance. If pelagic birding is an acquired taste, this kid had the wrong taste buds.

Worried the sickly, somber air would infect me, too, I ducked out and rejoined the throng. In the stern sat a weathered man in a full-brimmed hat and Hemingway beard. He was pulling fish guts out of a cooler and tossing them into water. Even in the wind, the oily fish aroma was overpowering.

"Looks chummy," said a guy in a puffy North Face jacket, winking at me. I forced a laugh.

"This obviously isn't your first rodeo," I said, turning to face him.

"My first rodeo?" He looked at me, perplexed.

"You're not from the states, are you?"

"India," he said. I felt dumb for missing his accent.

"What I meant was, have you been on a lot of these?"

"Not too many. I'm doing a post-doc at Old Dominion."

"Studying?"

"Acorn woodpeckers."

"Isn't Old Dominion in Virginia? Acorn woodpeckers don't live…"

"Right," he said, "that's why I'm here. Gotta return to India in three months. If I ever want to see seabirds, it's now or never."

The birds flying around the boat were as diverse as the bipedal mammals watching them. Albatrosses, petrels, fulmars, jaegers, skuas, and shearwaters came to the chum that Ernest Hemingway was pitching about. An ashy storm petrel drew parallel, dainty legs dangling as if its landing gear had jammed. It dabbed at a patina of fish oil and faded into the clouds like an escaped helium balloon. Two barrel-chested pomarine jaegers circled, greedy eyes noting every gobbet. A Northern fulmar, infamous for its ability to ward off predators with projectile vomit, sailed overhead. Unsure if the fulmar considered me a predator, I pulled on my hood.

Of all the aerial wizards, Debi's birds—the shearwaters—reigned supreme. Hundreds filled the sky while vast flotillas bobbed about the boat like peppercorns on a tossed salad. Unlike Alaska's sooty morph of the fox sparrow, the sooty shearwater didn't have any other varieties. All eighteen million sooty shearwaters around the globe appeared to have been dipped in dark chocolate. In front of us, they played chicken. Just before the bow threatened to squash them, they sprinted across the surface in a clumsy panic. In the sky, their grace returned. Aerial calligraphers, they sheared the water with their wingtips, stippling the surface.

Sooty shearwaters ceaselessly circle the globe. Despite the vast distances they travel, and the sameness of the featureless seas, shearwaters know where they are. A portion of their endocranial volume is devoted to the memory of one specific place, the particular patch of ground (underground, actually) their delicate feet first touch upon wiggling out of the eggshell. For ninety-seven days, freshly hatched shearwaters sit in the dark, at the end of dank, claustrophobic burrows dug into the flanks of small, rocky islands that rise off the coasts of New Zealand and Australia like gumdrops. To prevent being seen by predatory birds, shearwater parents drop out of the inky night sky with fishy deliveries.

Regurgitated fish guts can't last forever. To coax their young out, the parents cut their provisions, stretching the time between burrow appearances. Tummies rumbling, the hungry shearwaters waddle out, stretch their newly feathered wings, and pitch themselves into a headwind. Up, up, and away they go, their burrow, their little gumdrop island, disappearing below. The next six to nine years are a round-the-world odyssey, largely on the wing. They circle the blue planet to forage, rest, and for the few hundred around us, swoop around their greatest fan, Debi Shearwater.

Shearwaters, I noticed, lack hands. They lack pockets, fanny packs, and Lululemon shoulder bags, too. All navigational equipment—maps, GPS, compass, sextant, astrolabe—is stored in their brain. As acute as a security camera, those dinky bird brains miss nothing; ocular and olfactory data are perpetually filtered, processed and stored. They also detect a magnetosphere that our brains—1,400 cubic centimeters large—entirely miss. Shearwaters know where they are. Meanwhile, I wander out of Walmart and can't remember where I parked ten minutes earlier.

Shearwaters must find it insulting to share a kingdom with us, such navigational nincompoops. We share a kingdom with the birds, Animalia: The Latin root of "anima" meaning "breath" and "life." The miracle of movement—animation—separates us from the plants, though tumbleweed might beg to differ. We animals pick up our mats and walk. We aren't rooted yet many of us, like the shearwaters, remember our roots, no matter how long we've forsaken them. The farther we move away from our place of origin, the dearer it becomes. Moose Jaw, Mombasa, Scranton—no matter how remote, exotic, or forgettable, our birthplace stays with us. At least partially, it defines us, filling us with pride, or—depending on the place—embarrassment. "Where are you from?" I frequently ask. It matters.

We are a restless species. We grow up, move away, travel abroad, upsize, downsize, switch neighborhoods, change school districts, settle and uproot, moving an average of eleven times before settling permanently on the earth. Some of us forsake our birthplaces never to return. Not so with shearwaters. Though they sail the ocean blue, they never forsake that dank, claustrophobic burrow.

Not intentionally at least. On a late summer day in 1961, untold thousands of shearwaters descended inland to the shores of Monterey Bay, the very spot my pelagic cruise departed from. Their dependable, highly attuned navigational systems malfunctioned. Unable to discern land from water, they crash-landed, smacked into storefront windows and skidded down main street. Most died where they landed, wings splayed, necks twisted at grotesque angles. Delirious others swarmed the town in a deranged frenzy, coating surfaces with regurgitated anchovies. Mercifully, the apocalyptic plague ended quickly. Autopsies on the birds, and a few moribund sea turtles that also washed up, revealed the cause: Toxicity poisoning. An algal bloom biomagnified up the food chain, resulting in acute levels of toxicity—up to 79 percent—in the addled shearwaters.

Where some see misfortune, others see opportunity. Alfred Hitchcock was the latter. When he picked up the *Santa Cruz Sentinel* and perused the headline, a Grinchian smile spread across his face. I bet he took a long drag on his pipe and leaned back in his chair, the plot forming before him. Time was ripe for a new form of terror—winged terror. Two years later, *The Birds* debuted nationwide. Suspenseful and playing on deep-seated fears, the film became an instant classic.

My skin is too thin for horror. And since thrillers send my hyperhidrosis into overdrive, I long relegated *The Birds* to my things-to-avoid category, which includes poison ivy, black licorice, and neckties. During a stretch break in a recent ornithology class, the film crashlanded into my life. "You teach ornithology and haven't seen *The Birds?*" the class gasped in unison. "It's *masterful!*" The next week, one of my students handed me the film. Ugh. To appease, I popped it into my laptop after class and grabbed a stack of lab practicals. If I had to watch this "masterful" film, I'd at least get some grading done.

I finished one exam. In the middle of the second, my red pen slowed and then stopped altogether. It wasn't the film's action sequences that sucked me in, it was the lack thereof. This is no Marvel movie. Precious little happens. During one inexorably long spell of little action, Tippi Hedren, the protagonist, sits outside the Bodega Bay school and lights a cigarette. Tippi smokes and smokes, everything seemingly at peace. Music from a children's choir in a nearby school amplifies the darkening mood. Unbeknownst to Tippi, crows descend from the sky. They alight on the jungle gym bars in a deserted playground behind her. A few become dozens. Tippi finally senses them and grows agitated. A final crow lands, harbinger of the horror about to unfold.

By this point, ungraded exams were back on my desk. I was leaning forward in my chair, eyes wide. The climactic scene is as perfect as it is slow. Thrilling and cautionary, a reminder that we're not always in control, that nature can—and sometimes does—revolt. One minute you're whistling down Cannery Row. The next you're smacked upside the head by a deranged sooty shearwater.

Shearwaters aren't to blame for the Monterey Bay mayhem. Nor are the algae. Both were doing what they always do, plying the seas and utilizing nutrients. They're just easy scapegoats; we're the dunderheads. At the time of the incident, the California coast was experiencing a construction boom. Septic tanks were installed quickly. Some leaked, and the nutrients seeped into the to the bay. Avaricious algae gobbled them up and enjoyed a boom of their own. The toxicity amplified up the food chain, poisoning the fish and shearwaters that ate them. Crazed and disoriented, the birds lost their bearings, their lunch, and their lives.

On Debi's boat, I had lost my bearings not long after leaving the harbor. Worried I would regurgitate my lunch, I bid Hemingway and his chum adieu and shuffled back up to the bow. Booby lady was still there, more boisterous than ever. Her spat with Debi hadn't muted her.

"Rhinos! Three o'clock!" she shouted, pointing her binoculars at a raft of adorable rhinoceros auklets. Well named, white tufts that looked like horns projected upward from the base of their bills. "Pom jags, flying east!" Scanning with binoculars, all I saw was a mix of sky and sea. "Passerine! Passerine! Incoming! Twelve o'clock."

Passerine? Had the booby lady finally lost it? Passerines were songbirds, members of the vast Passeriformes order. It comprised over half the planet's bird species. Passerines had little in common with pelagics; they preferred sidewalk puddles to the mighty Pacific. What was a passerine doing out here?

Flying, apparently. So close I could have grabbed it, I found the bird as soon as I lowered my binoculars. The pocket-sized passerine made a pass over the boat, turned on a dime, and drew parallel. Curiously, it eyed us. Lacking confidence among these dedicated seadogs, I had yet to call out a bird. The pelagic birds had all been new. Not this fellow. I knew this passerine from my early days with my Golden Guide. Heck, if the booby lady could shout awkward things into the wind, so could I. "Butterbutt! Butterbutt!" I yelled, maniacally gleeful at this unexpectedly rich opportunity to mix sincerity with sarcasm.

Booby lady lowered her binoculars, crinkled her nose, and scowled. Contrary to what they say, imitation isn't always the sincerest form of flattery. "Yellow-rumped warbler," I clarified, grinning.

The bedraggled warbler flew with us for several seconds. Was it lost? I could have asked myself the same question.

Foolishly, hopefully, I extended my hand.

Coxswain

*A sailor who has charge of a
ship's boat and its crew and who
usually steers*

GOSHAWK

Few people head to polluted places to be inspired. But few people have the chance to do so with eighty-year-old Fleur Ng'weno, then chair of Nature Kenya, otherwise known as the East Africa Natural History Society. Through love of birds and dumb luck, the chance dropped in my lap. Coffee with Fleur would have sufficed; all day in Kenya's Lake Naivasha felt dreamlike. Ten zealous birders crowded into a canoe-shaped boat, tea-colored water sloshing around my shoes.

Fleur, hair as unruly as a weaver nest, sat in the bow as regal as a carved figurehead. I was squeezed in the middle with six, clipboard-toting Kenyan university students and one of my own. In the stern sat our captain, a grizzled Kenyan fisherman. Toothless, and apparently nameless, Fleur simply called him "coxswain." With hand motions I never decoded, she passed him a constant stream of signals. He smiled, whacked the faded engine cover with his palm, and pulled the rope start. We were off. Herons, kingfishers, and pelicans eyed our progress through the polluted waters teeming with hyacinth and hippos. More than enough to sink a ship, or a leaky boat.

My presence wasn't entirely dumb luck. I had volunteered to be part of a bird census, a country-wide endeavor to map the distribution of Kenya's bird species and assess their status. The data we recorded allowed conservationists to map population patterns and trends, critical for management initiatives. Data, I learned back in grad school, should never be taken for granted. Collecting it can be grueling, tedious, expensive, and in places like Africa, dangerous. Hippos are territorial. Boats capsize. A hippo's open maw was the last thing too many fishermen in this lake saw. Scary, yes, but the snorting hippos did help break the tedium of counting gray-hooded gulls, of which we eventually tallied 276. To spare expense and make the census possible, Fleur opted for discount boats, amiable fishermen, and amateur volunteers—suckers for punishment—us.

The sun was brutal. But not it, the hippos, or my now soaked shoes could have dampened my joy. Like my people in Monterey, this boatload of bird-loving, Swahili-chattering, coxswain-calling folks were my own. "I have nothing to say of my working life," Yann Martel wrote, "only that a tie is a noose, and inverted though it is, will hang a man if he's not careful." No ties or cubicles here. Just a fifty-two-square-mile lake of shining waters, a hefty dose of pollution, and a garnish of flamingos.

W̲ithout context and a history lesson, it would be easy for visitors—my students—to misunderstand the lake. It appeared pristine. Since things are rarely what they seem, I'd brought them to meet a curmudgeonly British expat named Don Turner, who lived on the lakeshore. Don had written a field guide, Birds of Kenya and Northern Tanzania, easier pulled by a wagon than carried. Neither Don, nor his anvil-heavy field guide, were short on bird knowledge. He wasn't short on opinions either. Now in his eighties, Don's politically incorrect, unfiltered monologue would educate my students far more memorably than I could.

"When I moved to Naivasha, there were seven thousand people scattered around the lake," Don said, frowning at my students. "Now there are 1.8 million." We clustered around him under the scant dappled shade of a fever tree. "Do you know what happens to everybody's crap? Every rain pumps it straight in." Don pointed toward the lake that shimmered just beyond us. "That's hardly the worst of it. All the herbicides and fertilizers from the flower fields go straight in too. You all heard of Teddy Roosevelt?" Heads nodded. "What do you think of him?"

"A great conservationist," I offered, unsure if any student knew, or cared, to answer.

"I call him an idiot," Don said, glaring at me. "Teddy dropped black bass into the lake because he thought they'd be fun to catch." I scribbled down Don's words, curious if a wee bit of anti-American bias was coloring his facts (It wasn't, it turns out.)

"He was hardly the only idiot," Don continued. "Other numb-skulls dumped crayfish and carp in, not to mention the South American hyacinth. It smothers everything. Look for yourselves." Heads swiveled toward the lake. Sure enough, a floating carpet of green and purple plants extended out from the shore. Don wasn't done. "Bet you haven't seen any native papyrus. That's because it's all been eaten by the cattle. Illegally, of course." Don worried a scab on his right arm as a breeze lifted the combed over ends of his wispy, white hair.

"We've sold our soul to China. They own us. Sixty-eight percent of our debt is owed to them. Do you know what happened when Zambia couldn't repay its loan? China took over their airport at Lusaka. When Angola defaulted, China seized their port. What will they take from us?" Don's gaze methodically moved from student to student. None dared speak. "Kenya can never pay this back. There's no tax base. Whatever taxes are collected goes straight to bloated civil servant salaries." Don's eyes locked on mine. "You know why I won't go in the water?"

"Why?" I asked.

"Because I know what's in it!"

Sophia, our winsome optimist from Fresno, hesitantly raised her hand. "Can Lake Naivasha ever be healed?"

"Impossible," Don said, snickering. "It's completely irreversible.

It will never return to what it was." Sophia eyes fell, her face ashen.

Unsure how much cynicism and sunburn my students could endure, I'd made today's bird census boat trip optional. Three had opted in, and Fleur, wanting to mix amateurs with experts, had split us up. While one puttered about the lake with me, the two others were bashing about the lakeshore in battered Land Cruisers. Learning some birds was a bonus; what I really wanted them to learn was how gifted our Kenyan counterparts were. In my boat I was outclassed immediately.

"Two yellow-billed ducks, six reed cormorants, one gray-hooded gull," Alfonse reported, binoculars scanning far-off snags.

"One pied kingfisher," Shukrani called out.

"I thought we were counting birds, not fish," chuckled Edrice. Shukrani lowered his binoculars and rolled his eyes.

"One mal-a-sheet-ay kingfisher," Rehema said, pointing to a dazzling little bird balancing midway up a slanted reed. I scanned the shore but failed to see it.

Fleur leaned over to Monica, who was recording the data on a clipboard. "Malachite kingfisher," she whispered, "not mal-a-sheet-ay." Little-used English pronunciations were Monica's only weakness.

"One great egret," I said, eager to contribute. Eagle-eyed Alfonse redirected his gaze.

"Actually, one intermediate egret," he corrected. "The gape line stops at the eye." I relocated the bird I had confidently announced. Sure enough, the little yellow line that extended from the bill stopped abruptly at the bird's eye. With a look of endearment and professionalism, Alfonse explained: "With the great egret, the gape line extends through the eye."

Alfonse's tone wasn't patronizing, but his corrective stung nonetheless. Other than Fleur, I had naively assumed I'd be the best birder in the boat. I was twice as old as these students, had published papers, and had a fancy PhD in ecology. I had birded my whole life, but obviously not long enough. The bird was an intermediate egret, and I was an intermediate birder.

Skin burnt, feet waterlogged, and ego deflated, I turned to note-taking. I had ground to make up and there was no time like the present. "One purple heron," Fleur said, pointing aft. I studied the elegant bird, resting on one leg in a nearby snag. 'Purple heron, cinnamon-colored not purple,' I scrawled.

"Four flamingos swimming," interjected Edrice. Swimming? Sure enough, beyond a basketball court-sized patch of hyacinth were four flamingos, impersonating swans in the deep water. 'Flamingos swim like ducks,' I wrote, and then added: 'Pied kingfishers hover like hummingbirds.' Epiphanies abounded. Out here, I was a student. Maybe I would be forever.

"Let's push up along that stand of papyrus," Fleur said, pointing right of the flamingos. "I'd like to see if anything's using it." Our boat had drifted into the hyacinth. With two heavily calloused hands, the coxswain futilely tried to untangle the propeller. Unable, he lifted the outboard—plants and all—out of the water, grabbed a pole, and pushed us ahead like a Venetian gondolier. "A first-rate coxswain," Fleur remarked, grabbing the gunwales to steady herself.

Fleur was first-rate, too. As a child, she traveled extensively due to her father's work with the United Nations. In 1963, she came to Kenya, married Hilary Ng'weno, and raised a family. Her interest in wildlife grew steadily. Weekly, she led bird walks on the grounds of the Nairobi Museum and nearby Uhuru Park. As Kenya developed and the population swelled, Fleur realized the importance of conservation. Bird populations needed to be assessed and monitored, and the rarest species needed protection.

The Clarke's weaver was one of Kenya's rarest endemics, and quickly caught her attention. During her monitoring efforts, Fleur noticed that the weaver, first described in 1913 along the northeast coast, would periodically disappear from the Arabuko Sokoke Forest. Together with A Rocha Kenya, she realized that nobody knew where the weaver bred and nested. But there was one important clue: Back in 1994, Don Turner, the sour grapes straightshooter who spoke to my students, had found a flock of Clarke's weavers further inland in the Dakatcha Woodlands.

The Dakatcha Woodlands are not on Kenya's safari circuit. It's a hot, dry region marked by ethnic unrest. Difficult to access, Fleur realized she needed local assistance. She immediately set to work and built capacity with local communities, which evolved into the Dakatcha Woodland Conservation Group. The group began regular bird surveys in the woodlands. Finally, her work paid off. On March 22, 2013, exactly one hundred years after the weaver was first described, Fleur and her team spied nests in a small area of wetland. They monitored the birds, and eventually uncovered nearly five hundred nests. By April 19, the colony fledged a new cohort of young and abandoned the nesting grounds. The data became a technical paper, published in *Scopus,* phlegmatically entitled: *"First recorded breeding of Clarke's weaver Ploceus golandi. "*

It may not seem like much, tantamount to a team of astronomers discovering another moon on Neptune. But conservationists were elated. Intent on protecting the rarest and most vulnerable, the discovery was critical. Without protecting nesting grounds, there is no nesting. Data collection—tedious, grueling, expensive, and dangerous—underlies it all.

"Coxswain, usiendi zaidi," Fleur said in a unique Victorian English-Swahili blend. Unable to hear Fleur's thin voice, the coxswain cupped his ear. Fleur reverted to hand signals and motioned him to stop. "Seems we have an uptick in reed cormorants and Egyptian geese," she said, raising her binoculars for the umpteenth time. Alfonse dutifully called out totals to Monica.

"I thought so," she said, scanning a cluster of globular nests hanging from sagging papyrus stalks. They looked like oversized ornaments on Charlie Brown trees. Each nest was intricately woven. On the underside, entrance holes faced downward, more effective for warding off rain and predators. But their architectural cleverness wasn't enough.

WHOOSH! A raptor struck the colony like a cruise missile. Pandemonium detonated causing hysterical weavers exploded in every direction. The raptor hopped among the nests, searching for accessible young. Sensing vulnerability, it hooked its talons into a nest and flipped upside-down, a master of avian parkour. Flapping for balance, the hungry predator probed one long metatarsal into the entrance hole.

"One gabar goshawk," Fleur called out wryly, before adding: "Whatever number of village weavers we come up with, we'll have to subtract one." On cue, the goshawk pulled out a plump, pink nestling. Grass and feather-linings showered into the lake like confetti. Clutching its prize, the goshawk sped off to dine in peace.

"'Tis a perfect time for tea and bitings," Fleur said, eyes twinkling. "Shukrani, please fetch the cooler." The cooler, now floating in two inches of water and banging the poor coxswain's knees, was fetched and the bitings—meat and veggie samosas—were distributed. Fleur kept birding while we refortified. "One little bittern," she said, binoculars trained on a shadowy bit of shoreline. I studied the shore but again couldn't find the bird. Fleur noticed my frustration. "Do you see the one hyacinth in bloom?" She asked, "The one with the purple flower?" I nodded. "Directly behind it." Indeed. The little bittern came into focus.

Fleur came into focus, too. Her eighty-year-old eyes missed little. "All true meaning resides in the personal relationship to a phenomenon," Chris McCandless penned as his life ebbed away on his ill-fated sojourn in the Alaskan wilderness. McCandless's sentiment isn't unique. Fleur understood. But she discovered it less tragically, through systematic, dedicated observation. Don Turner did, too. Both Fleur and Don had lived much of their lives in Kenya. They loved Lake Naivasha and its birdlife. What differed is how they expressed their love. Don had seen enough. For him, the game was over. Fleur could never see enough. She would always keep looking.

Hours later, our dependable coxswain coaxed our half-submerged bathtub back to shore. Data collected; part of the annual bird census was complete. Satisfied, I sloshed out notebook in hand. My notes were shorthand and trivial: The length of the gape line on an intermediate egret, purple herons aren't purple, flamingos swim like ducks, pied kingfishers can hover.

Tiny details of little significance. But on another level, the details mattered, representative of a better, more careful way of seeing—of living. Hungry for more, I stepped out of the boat feeling different. I was a goshawk; focused and intent, probing the world for all that it offered.

Zugunruhe

Anxious behavior in migratory animals, especially in birds, experienced at the beginning of the normal migration period.

Many birds migrate at night. To study the phenomenon during the spring and fall, meddling scientists hold birds in little, round cages overnight. Slightly inclined walls, coated in scratch-sensitive paper, surround the birds. Marks on the paper record the bird's orientation and fluttery movements. They record the direction the bird wants to go. Findings from these Emlen funnels are telling. Iron deposits in each captive's head aligns with the Earth's magnetic field, instructing the birds where to go. Placed in the funnels in spring, the birds orient northward. In the fall, southward. They scratch away at the walls, raring to go. Migratory birds, the funnels reveal, know their cardinal directions.

Trapped in my restless, pun-loving body, I scratch away at my own walls. But, unless it's sunrise or sunset, I am hopeless with cardinal directions. Unlike the birds, direction has been hard for me to find. Without much, at age twenty, I went to Africa.

Chicken pox forced me to finish my sophomore year of college at home. In a shivering delirium, I rolled over and stared at the faded world map I had taped to my wall during high school. The map had hung so long I had ceased to notice it. Now the vast continent of Africa, fifty-odd countries large, sat five inches from my stuffy nose. Too cold and weak to get out of bed, I studied Africa for five straight days.

A year later, I landed in Tanzania, a participant in my university's three-month study abroad semester. The chicken pox was long gone and now, eager for experiential learning, my prolonged academic stupor was about to disappear too. No more overhead projectors, windowless classrooms, and predictable lectures. The Africa program was better than advertised. To learn history, we visited stone age sites and ran our hands over intricately carved doors in Zanzibar. In anthropology "class", we slept in rural village homes and hung out with Maasai pastoralists. For biology, we clung to roof racks and drove through teeming herds of wildlife.

In between outings, we pitched tents, spread out sleeping bags, and a handful of my peers rested. I went birding. Colorful birds were everywhere, especially so at one idyllic campsite, Masumbo, where we stayed for several weeks. In the local language, "masumbo" referred to the place "where water flows over the rocks." The name was apt. Mocha-colored water swirled around granitic, sedan-sized boulders as a river—the Little Ruaha—carved through the red earth. Bamboo and eucalyptus groves adorned the verdant banks, a playground for troops of vervet monkeys and a shadowy refuge for pythons and puff adders.

Our semester coincided with rainy season. The swollen river, home to a rogue hippo, added drama to our nocturnal trips to the outhouse by shearing grass around our tents at night. I mostly resisted the temptation to swim. I never resisted the temptation to watch birds along the Ruaha's shady banks.

There was much to watch. Weavers lined the reeds with nests, bee-eaters sallied over the water, wagtails waltzed about the mud, and every so often, a giant kingfisher, the largest of its kind, strafed the surface with a machine gun rattle. Ever since I had spied the chestnut-sided warbler in Pennsylvania, my interest in birds had metastasized. Here they seemed bigger, louder, crazier, and more abundant. In the States, I looked for birds. In Tanzania, it seemed, they looked for me.

All but one, that is—the African finfoot. I had greeted the finfoot many times in my *Birds of East Africa* field guide, but never in the flesh. It swam across the bottom of plate eight, larger and more exquisite than the others. It had a long neck, aquiline body, and sharp, bicolored bill—a duck on a diet plan, or the offspring of a swan and a snake. Its feet, as its name suggested, were lobed, more finlike than weblike. I fixated on the finfoot. Whatever "it" was, the finfoot had it in spades.

The field guide's description heightened my desire to find one: "Singles and pairs are uncommon, secretive and may be overlooked." Addictive traits for a first-time seeker, my finfoot craving began. Overlook them I wouldn't.

Active pursuit worked for most birds, not so with the finfoot. Since the bird was secretive, letting one find me was the best—maybe only—approach. I had to sit at the ready, long patient vigils my only real chance. Every spare minute of the semester, I crept to the river and settled among the bamboo. Sacred idleness brought me squeaky paradise flycatchers, mournful tambourine doves, and chatty yellow-bellied greenbuls. But if an African finfoot paddled past me with those lovely, lobate toes, I missed it.

I soon missed Africa too. The semester ended. Back in the states, I no longer took electricity, faucets, and car suspension for granted. I missed it all. The immersive learning, campfire stories, pounding rain showers, and softball-sized avocados. I missed the people and wildlife, the joyful laughter around the flickering light of a kerosene lantern, and my long finfootless vigils by the river. Africa gave me direction. I had to get back. But how?

My predicament was borne of zugunruhe—restlessness. A feeling one writer likens to "runners loosening up before a marathon." One thing I knew: If I ever made a triumphal return to Africa, it had to involve wildlife. To do that, degrees would help. I finished college, dove into a master's degree in environmental science, and got married, all the while hoping Africa would call me back.

The call came.

"Eli, Jon Arensen here. Are you ready to come to Africa?" he asked immediately, foregoing pleasantries. I was in Santa Barbara, putting the finishing touches on my master's. I had studied under Jon during my glorious Tanzania semester. Now, he was in New York, from whence he was planning another study abroad semester with Houghton University.

"What would my role be?" I asked, giddy with the possibility of return.

Jon had grown up in Africa. He spoke several languages, was as tan as a lion's mane, and loved wildlife as much as I did. With this invitation, I had the chance to shadow him and learn his secrets.

"Run logistics," Jon said. "Scout new places for me. Help me teach the wildlife course. Teach about birds. You know them better than I do." I doubted this. But I would have gone, whatever role Jon described.

"I'd love to but there's this …," I paused, wondering if I should even mention the PhD program I'd applied to months earlier. Jon waited. Oh well, I'd have to tell him eventually. I plunged ahead. "Colorado State has a research opportunity to study human-wildlife issues in the Serengeti National Park. I doubt I'll get accepted, and I'm not sure when the starting date would …"

"Serengeti?" Jon interrupted. "Chased gazelles there once. Ran them down with flashlights. Jumped on their backs."

"You jumped on gazelles in the Serengeti?" I asked. "For fun?"

"Research," Jon answered. "You'll get accepted. Don't worry about dates. We'll make it work."

Jon's words proved prophetic. We made it work. Jon did the heavy lifting. Once or twice a week, I took students on bird walks or lectured, convinced that concepts like brood parasitism and reverse sex polyandry would change their lives. When not teaching, I sat in the back of Jon's classes memorizing his stories, determined to one day teach as effectively. (Spoiler alert: I haven't).

One day, while Jon told a story about the battle for Lake Tanganyika during World War I, my eyes strayed over the spreading limbs of the stout acacia that shaded our thatched-roof classroom. Subconsciously scanning, my gaze fell upon a fist-sized knob I hadn't noticed before. From my seat in the back, the knob appeared to be the base of a branch that had broken off at its point of attachment. Curious, I raised my binoculars. "Dr. Arensen," I interrupted. Jon nodded, looking at me over the rim of his glasses. "Can I show the class a Eurasian nightjar?" Jon's eyebrows went up.

"Where?"

"There." I pointed to the limb.

"Sure. Great stopping point. We'll pick up history next week. Let's shift to Eli's class."

Students looked at each other, confusion in their eyes. They hadn't completely transitioned from typical classrooms yet. How did the battle of Lake Tanganyika end up? What was a nightjar? What was this program where one course bled abruptly into another? Curiosity quickly won out. They closed their notebooks, pulled out binoculars, and happily shuffled out the classroom door.

This was how school was supposed to be: stimulating, flexible, and opportunistic. If a classroom experience could be like this, and not the usual hamster wheel of monotone lectures followed by hours of busywork, maybe I could teach too.

After my impromptu lesson about nightjars and optimal foraging strategies, I went down to the river to resume the finfoot watch I had begun as a student. Field guide across my lap, I read the description for the hundredth time. The finfoot prefers "permanent rivers, streams and pools with overhanging vegetation." What the field guide didn't say was why cover was so essential. My reading led to another discovery: The finfoot was a member of the Heliornithidae, a small family with just three members: the masked finfoot of Southeast Asia, the sun-grebe of South America, and the African finfoot, the wholly African species that despite untold hours on the riverbank, eluded me yet again.

—

Five years later, I was at Colorado State having completed several years in Serengeti studying how the park impacted the people who lived around it. I bent over my desk in a noisy, third-floor apartment, typing out the final chapter of my dissertation. My funding was spent, I was spent, and our first child—Ezra—was squirming in the crib next to me. Rap music throbbed through the walls of the apartment next door. The US economy was in recession. Employees were let go. Opportunities were scarce. I had few prospects and yet again in my life, little direction. I was staring out the window when the phone rang.

"Eli, Jon Arensen here. Are you ready to come back to Africa?"

True to form, he didn't waste time on pleasantries.

"Logistics?" I asked, disbelieving my luck.

"No. To take over the program."

"What do you..." Jon didn't let me finish.

"I'm getting on up there. Can't teach forever. The dean asked me to make a transition plan. You're it."

"A transition plan?" I asked, goosebumps rising on my arms.

"From me to you. When I retire, the Africa program is yours." Like his prior life-altering phone call, this was an order more than an invitation. Ezra gurgled and rolled over. I shut my laptop and stood up.

"I haven't finished my dissertation," I faltered, head spinning with possibility.

"Doesn't matter. To me or the dean. Finish it after you get here."

"When would you want me to start?"

"January."

"When do I apply?"

"Not sure. The president's going to call you next week. She'll work that out."

For Jon, everything always worked out. Africa was too big for details. Deals were sealed with head nods and handshakes.

"Wait. Are you really retiring?" I asked.

Jon hadn't lost a step; I couldn't imagine him not teaching.

"Not for a few years. Will be fun to overlap. Should make the handoff easier."

"Wow. Thanks!" I said, before adding, "I should really talk this over with Linda."

"Of course. Can't wait to have you two back, now that Africa's in your blood."

Jon was right: Africa was in my blood now. My Serengeti years had been baptism by fire, but I had emerged a true convert. With Linda alongside, we had plowed our arthritic Land Rover through flooded rivers, collected boxfuls of data, played Scrabble by candlelight in our plumbing-free, electricity-free, but not-baboon-free research house, climbed Mount Kilimanjaro, and drifted off at night to the roar of lions. Able to speak Swahili, I now had African friends and treasured the little red paths that slithered through the bush. Zugunruhe had led me to Africa; I had learned my path of migration.

I took the job, assumed a professorship in New York, and squeaked out a dissertation. As Jon's successor, we—my little family and a quorum of students—traveled to Africa every year. The job was demanding but not without perks: Teeth-chattering winters were no more, twenty-five college students could babysit, and we shared an unpredictable life that precluded boredom. Teaching was ancillary to my semester's main objective: return with the same number of students I departed with.

Thankfully, we did. But over time, the costs of our exciting nomadic life surfaced: Friendships were transitory without the sinew of consistency. Yearly commune-style living with students tested our patience. Students got sick. We got sick. Credit cards failed. Phone connections were spotty. Networks went down. Bookings fell through. Cars broke. Roads washed away. Heat withered resolve.

Raised in Africa, Jon handled these challenges effortlessly. Raised in America, I not so much. Jon knew where he belonged. I battled another case of Zugunruhe.

—

One semester, with a dozen under my belt, I walked wearily down to the river. Constant travel had worn me down, and this year's student group had bad chemistry. They rankled at our attempts to untether them from Wi-Fi and had complained about the homestays we arranged. Our aging vehicles showed their years, and a variety of sicknesses had knocked us down like dominoes. With recent political unrest in Tanzania, I had started to investigate other field sites, other countries, even other professions.

Jon had retired. Without his counsel and charismatic presence, thoughts of throwing in the towel bubbled up. I wove around a bamboo grove, pulled out a moth-nibbled camp chair I'd stashed, and settled in, camera bag by my side and a cup of steaming chai cradled in my hands. Swirling, sediment-laden eddies roiled around, foam pirouetting in the middle. On the other side, several golden-backed weavers clambered atop bent-over stalks of elephant grass, green streamers dangling from their bills. To my left, on a desiccated bamboo stem, sat a pair of little bee-eaters, body-to-body, unheedful of personal space. One launched, missed an invisible bug, and returned. As penance, it preened the other. "We see that the miraculous is not extraordinary," Wendell Berry wrote. "It is our daily bread."

But the next moment was miraculous and extraordinary. Red. A bill. An eye. A serpentine neck. Just across the frothing river, a finfoot snaked out of a tangle of elephant grass. A second followed. Finfoots! Silently, the two half-submerged birds shapeshifted upriver. A purist would have relished the moment with folded hands. Unpure, I grabbed my camera, tossed the lens cap aside and squeezed off one photo a moment before they melted into the vegetation.

Years later, I had it printed. Ill-composed, underexposed, and shadowy, it remains my most cherished photograph.

Another African migration finished, I pulled into the long, gravel driveway that led to a log cabin set above a small, cattail-lined pond. Since retirement, Jon and his wife, Barb, had lived in this rustic, safari-themed home, partly so Jon could watch game from his windows. When not overseas, Linda and I had purchased a nondescript little house on a creek just a few miles down the dead-end road. For health reasons, Jon's retirement decision proved serendipitous. Not long after retirement, both he and Barb developed Parkinson's disease, with unpleasant and debilitating symptoms.

I was eager to tell Jon about my finfoot sighting, to talk Africa, and to see if I could help out with anything. As usual, Jon spied me approaching, gave me a hearty Swahili greeting, and led me inside. In the context of rural western New York, the Arensen house stood out. It was a museum. Reed-woven Sudanese baskets lined the floors, seashells from the South Pacific filled display cases, and a Cape buffalo skull spanned the living room wall. Jon walked stiffly and braced himself on the back of a chair.

"How are you holding up?" I asked, settling on the couch. I was hopeful his latest round of medications was warding off his constant pain.

"Not sleeping much," Jon said, meeting my eye. "Can't feel my extremities. But I'm writing, doing art." He never lingered on his growing list of ailments. "Hey, I've got a book for you." He shuffled over to his bookshelf and pulled one out with a worn, faded cover. "It's about a family who carved out a living in the Karoo desert of South Africa." He handed it to me. "Full of hardships the family endures, but they fall in love with the place." He paused by a window and looked out at the pond. I cradled his autobiography in my hands.

Diagnosis is cheap, the saying goes, but remedy is expensive. As one season blended into another, the remedy for Jon and Barb crystallized on one option: a final migration back to Africa. Time was running out and Jon was restless for a final adventure, a return to his land of golden joys. On an otherwise ordinary Saturday morning, my phone rang. It was a call I'd never forget.

"Eli, Jon Arensen here."

My mind flashed back to the other times Jon had called, each one personally seismic and life-shaping. I braced myself. As usual Jon didn't mince words—but the assistance he asked for this time was physical, not vocational.

"What's up?" I asked.

"Need you to bury the cat."

"Molly?"

"Afraid so. Barb discovered her this morning on the laundry room floor. Can't pick her up. Hands don't work anymore."

"Be right over."

A kaleidoscope of crisp October leaves blew around our ankles as I jabbed the shovel into the dry earth just beyond the edge of their yard. The interment felt like the final leg of our long and gratifying journey together. At critical junctures, Jon had given me direction and purpose. Our lives had coiled around each other's for decades. This burial ceremony was symbolic, but hardly solemn.

"Don't dig too deep," Jon said, peering into the hole. "We don't want to make the bears work too hard for their midnight snack."

"You're heartless, Jon," Barb said, cuffing him on the back.

"Never had to bury many pets in Africa," Jon quipped. "Leopards got them first."

A year later, Linda and I stood in Jon's driveway with their daughter, Lisa. All their belongings had been given away to friends and family. Jon had already sold the house through a backchannel, via a handshake with a friend as was his custom. For years, the house had provided convenience, amenities, and easy access to healthcare. But it wasn't home.

Rain drizzled down as Lisa helped her parents into the car that would take them to the airport with one-way tickets to Africa. Jon slid his passenger window down. He met our faces with an ear-to-ear grin. Fighting tears, I couldn't muster anything. Jon could. "The last safari!" he called out, as the car eased away.

Migration complete, Jon sent out a message not long after his return to Africa:

> Thanks to all of you who made kind comments about our new home in Kenya. It will take some time as we settle into the change in routine. The first day the electricity went off. This blew the water pump so no water in the house. Then the car broke down on the way to buy parts. We know we are back in Africa.

Jon has returned to the land that formed him. A land where limitless joy and soul fusion override daily inconvenience. A land of the finfoot. I'm eternally grateful the African finfoot—Jon—swam into the open and entered my life when he did. And I'm grateful he has retired back into cover. To a place his soul belongs, where deeper rest can be found. A place where a leopard can take him first.

Commensalism

A relation between two kinds of organisms in which one obtains food or other benefits from the other without damaging or benefiting it

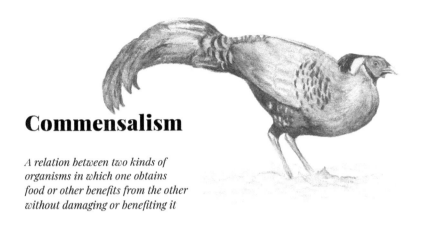

SIAMESE FIREBACK

Perfect foils for finfoots, one needn't sit quietly for months on end to see the house sparrow. One needn't use binoculars, or, for that matter, even walk outside. They're indoorsy, equally at home in any airport, Home Depot, or food court. In ecological language, this makes them invasive. While house sparrows are surely that, I prefer to highlight a redemptive quality of these oft-benighted birds: House sparrows choose to dine with us. Wholly commensal, they have forsaken their native lands—Asia, North Africa, and Europe—to follow humanity around the globe, nesting in our buildings and finishing our French fries. Homeowners and ecologists can hate, but humans are the central character of the house sparrow's story. *Passer domesticus* is innocent; we have abetted their travel lust, having introduced them to new locations no fewer than 250 times.

I can proudly report that I have never introduced a house sparrow—but I have introduced flocks of students to locations all around the globe. I have incited their lust for travel, most often to Africa. Recently, I accompanied two of my most intrepid to a location I had no familiarity with: A remote ecotourism camp in the backcountry hills of Cambodia, bordering Vietnam. The job called for two years of service and offered everything that young, environmentally minded students could want: adventure, a chance to put knowledge into practice, learn a new language, work with local people, and for a few weeks, host the conniving professor who had encouraged them.

I arrived in Phnom Penh with the intentions of a house sparrow, eager to dine with my students and live among them. In exchange for language help and a tent, I promised I would stand to the side and let them roll. Entertaining myself was gravy; Cambodia has plenty of birds. At Wat Phnom, a Buddhist temple complex in the heart of the bustling city of over two million, house sparrows—unsurprisingly—were the first birds I watched.

House sparrows may choose to dine with us, but these don't choose to cram into little cages with dozens of scruffy manakins. Their captors were profit-minded sellers. The sparrows flew at the wooden bars in protest of imprisonment. Incense hung in the treacly air as musicians, mendicants, and saffron-robed monks rested amid castellated crannies. A man, hair pulled back in a white, wiry ponytail, walked up to a stooped, old woman leaning against the temple wall. He dropped a few coins into her outstretched, leathery hand. She unlatched the door, pulled out a bird and gingerly handed it to him. He cupped it, bowed slightly, and lobbed it skyward. A freeing act—'sawab'—conferred spiritual merit. The pilgrim tottered off.

I was less certain about my own spiritual merit. An academic pilgrim weary of traditional classroom learning, I favored the experiential. My own experiences abroad as a student had fundamentally changed me. They made book learning relevant, widened my perspective, and seared formative moments like a branding iron. I patterned my life on it now, taking students along and sending them out.

But as a trapped house sparrow knows, a love of novelty—an attachment to a new mode of living—comes with a cost. So connected have house sparrows become to us, ecologists regard them as anthro-dependent. It has given the adaptable birds a leg—wing—up for now. But studies have shown that some human-associated populations of house sparrows were extirpated not long after people moved away from a particular location. Was I consigning my students to a similar fate? Were these exotic opportunities increasing their vulnerabilities? What were the costs?

"Most vertebrates are either fearful of strange objects or indifferent to them," writes Jennifer Ackerman in *The Genius of Birds*, "but newfangledness of most kinds doesn't seem to faze a house sparrow." They have another noteworthy accolade: Other than people, house sparrows are the first documented species to be drawn to novel objects. Ecological physiologist Lynn Martin conducted a clever experiment: Akin to the Emlen funnels used to measure migratory restlessness, Martin inserted unfamiliar objects—a rubber ball, a toy plastic lizard—placing them near seed-filled cups in a small aviary containing several different species. The objects aroused apathy or fear in every species bar one: house sparrows. The brazen little birds hopped right over to investigate, seemingly energized. "If you're going to invade a new place," Ackerman explains, "a love of novelty helps."

Love of novelty or not, house sparrows had yet to invade Jahoo Gibbon Camp, a fledgling ecotourism destination in a remnant scrap of Cambodian jungle. The steamy jungle had too many dangers for the civilized sparrows, and plenty for humans to consider, too. I was contemplating the tradeoffs of travel, staying out of my students' way, and, of course, watching birds.

Noticing my damp shirt and binoculars, one of the local Bunong guides who worked at the camp, Hong, approached me. "You want walk jungle at night?" he asked. He and another guide, Salah, were learning English. Hikes with English speakers meant more practice for them. I didn't hesitate.

"Yes!"

"You no care if rain?"

"Not at all," I fibbed. I would go, but watching birds is hard in the rain. "Can we go every night?" I asked. Hong smiled, nodding. Most of the camp's clients went just once. In this case, I wasn't a house sparrow in it for the novelty. I wanted repeated interaction—connection—and as much as I could get.

At nightfall, we entered the jungle single file. Used to the longer sightlines afforded by temperate forests and African savannas, the inky rainforest felt claustrophobic. I couldn't see beyond the small orb of light cast by my headlamp. Raindrops pattered down, cascading through leafy cataracts. Hong stopped, his beam trained on a bush. Like an actor on stage, a fluffy dollop of blue perched in the spotlight. "Siberian blue robin," Salah said, resuming his search. We stepped over trees and around rain-slicked rocks. Salah tapped Hong's shoulder and motioned with his flashlight beam. Wrapped around a liana vine—apparently—was a snake. "Mock viper," he said blandly, as if such snakes were as common as park pigeons. I stared at the vine but saw nothing. "Come on," Kyle whispered, "You'll see plenty more of them." Kyle was one of the students I'd encouraged to work at Jahoo. He was dark-haired, sturdy, and dependable. Clearly, he'd grown used to the snakes. I hadn't.

"Where?" I asked. Hong picked a stick off the ground and pointed. "Here," he said, wiggling the tip of the stick. "Is brown," I still couldn't find it. Sensing this, he stepped forward and poked the viper. Suddenly, what I had mistaken for the vine slithered upward. It had a triangular head and tan, finger-thin body. "Now you see?"

I saw. I also saw that this viper, mock or not, was small enough to curl up in my sneaker or camera bag. I would shake things out going forward.

"Takes time to see," Hong said, resuming our walk. He made it sound so simple.

"How did they learn all this?" I asked Kyle.

"They grew up walking these trails," he said, shrugging. While it took time to learn the jungle, I sensed it took interest, too, something akin to love. I had met too many people who only saw the birds that hit their windows.

The jungle was like Las Vegas; experiencing it at night was entirely different. But unlike the Las Vegas nightlife, some of the most colorful characters dozed: Black-naped monarchs, hainan flycatchers, orange-breasted trogons, and a groggy banded kingfisher that I could have plucked from its perch. Other creatures were more active: Gliding lizards, whip scorpions, palm-sized snails, and a bug-eyed mammal that looked like the dumpy love child of Gollum and a pet guinea pig.

"Pygmy slow loris," Salah said, as the creature blinked uncomfortably in the beam. I scrawled the animal's name into my notebook. Political correctness was obviously a latecomer to mammalian nomenclature.

"There!" Hong interrupted, grabbing my forearm. A knee-high deer with pencil legs melted away before I could raise my camera. "Lesser Oriental chevrotain," he said, pronouncing the multisyllabic name slowly.

"Lesser slow American," I said, pointing to myself. Used to dumb comments by pale dunderheads, Hong and Salah ignored me.

Two frogs and a footlong centipede later, Salah halted our progress with a raised palm. I had given up trying to spot things before they did. Now their separate beams converged on a branch in the canopy: In the spotlight sat a funky chicken. Cobalt wings, shapely tail, mullet, and a face that looked like a flattened strawberry. The bird would fit in at a county fair. Hong smiled.

"Siamese fireback," he said. "Male." I furrowed my brow. The bird's back was decidedly unfiery; fireface seemed more appropriate. Hong noticed my raised eyebrow. "Yellow," he said, pointing to his own back. He looked at Salah, obviously hunting for an English.

"Yellow is hidden," Salah added.

Unless pointed out by my guides, everything was hidden. Or, like the birds I'd been shown, over my head. Back in my tent that night, I flipped open my field guide to the Siamese fireback. Sure enough, the male's back was yellow-orange, likely to impress females. On its face were large caruncles or, according to the text: 'fleshy excrescence.'

My brain was a fleshy excrescence. I couldn't take credit for any of the creatures I'd seen. I could only take credit for a willingness to venture out of my comfort zone, stumble around a dank Cambodian jungle at night, and follow the flashlight beams of two sharp-eyed experts. Small sacrifices. Out here, novelty was well worth taking risks for.

I feel far more comfortable in Africa than Asia. I should. I studied there, did graduate research, and jostled around the continent in beat-up Land Cruisers—and a fair number of leaky boats. The longer I spent, the more I noticed. Most conspicuous was how my students adjusted to a new place. For some, it was love at first sight; they were drawn to hospitable people, charismatic wildlife, and go-with-the-flow experiential learning. Others, with a penchant for schedules, order, and control, quickly crossed Africa off their list. I noticed a third group as well, students who underwent a metamorphosis. These adaptable few relinquished their desire for control and predictability. They gradually let themselves go and fell into Africa's embrace. Varied reactions that proved remarkably similar to those of house sparrows that first arrived on the Kenyan coast.

House sparrows first arrived in Mombasa (introduced by people, of course) in the 1950s. Being house sparrows, they immediately followed human settlement as it spread inland. Today, the cities they inhabit stretch westward to Uganda. Lynn Martin, the same clever researcher who dropped novel objects into bird aviaries, caught wild birds from various subpopulations and recorded their vitals. His results were revealing. The most adventurous birds, those on the leading edge of the range expansion, released the greatest amount of stress hormone—corticosterone—upon being caught than did those from subpopulations that hadn't traveled far.

When I first encountered Martin's research, it seemed counterintuitive. Wouldn't the most daring house sparrows, I reasoned, stress out the least? Wouldn't they take risk taking in stride? In *The Genius of Birds*, Jennifer Ackerman suggests that greater stress hormone release may imbue the birds with more flexibility and quicken their reaction times to unforeseen danger. It may improve their memories of dangerous situations, too.

Martin's grad student, Andrea Liebl, took house sparrow experiments one step farther. She exposed individuals from the various subpopulations to foreign foods, like freeze-dried strawberries. Though they'd never encountered such foods, sparrows on the leading edge, the daring ones, swallowed them with alacrity. More established populations, those less willing to travel, didn't touch the exotic fare.

As a whole, house sparrows aren't afraid to light out for the territory, but there's much variation within the collective. While rewards may come on the leading edge, there can be wisdom in hanging back. Foods can be toxic. New places carry risks that can be difficult to assess. A snake—a mock viper, say—might be lurking in a liana.

I don't know whether it's wiser to stay or go either. While trying new things is part of growing up, maybe not so quickly, or so routinely. Maybe it's all context dependent, or just another false dichotomy brewed up by western thinking. I'm not sure.

But I am sure that vision—the ability to see things others don't—can be acquired both ways. Whether I stay or go, for however long, I want to see as Hong and Salah see—the lizards, lorises, and chevrotains. I want to see well enough and watch long enough for vision to become knowledge. I don't want to be told what a Siamese fireback is, I want to recognize it. Instantly. Looks can be deceiving, even though the fireback appears to blue, it can part its wings and ignite.

I hope it's not too late. The tonic of travel has bewitched me with novelty and kept me on the move. For all I've yet to learn, my travels in an inky, wet Cambodian jungle have taught me this: It takes time to see. And, like a house sparrow, willingness to follow another's lead.

Munificence

*The quality or action of being
lavishly generous; great generosity*

PUERTO RICAN PARROT

To go far in academia, you often need unhealthy amounts of three things: ambition, perseverance, and skepticism. Set your sights high. Keep going. Question all research. (Except your own, of course.) These three traits slipped into my ornithology courses, too, as manifested on a recent trip to Puerto Rico. For me, the island offered a rich place to play hide-and-seek with the endemic birds. For my students, an easy chance to procure a few science credits without donning a lab coat. Morning hours for the birds, balmy afternoons for the beach? Yes, please. The roster filled up quickly.

Puerto Rico is tame compared to other places I've taken students. Just a short flight from Miami, we could get around with occasional Wi-Fi, Google maps, and broken Spanish. Get around, perhaps, but not see all the birds. "We aren't going to see all the island's endemics," I told my students matter-of-factly a few days before the trip. "We won't see the Puerto Rican owl and have no chance at the Puerto Rican parrot." The little research I'd done showed both to be a little too particular to place. The owl remained motionless all day in dense cover, and the parrot was restricted to two tiny forest fragments. Finding either required a focused solo mission without regular meals and bathroom breaks, not a parade of quasi-interested, small-bladdered, yap-happy undergrads. Since the students weren't even aware of the two species before I brought them up, not seeing them didn't matter; most had signed up for all the time we wouldn't be birding.

While the owls' population was healthy, the parrots' was not; its freefall alarming. Many parrot populations around the world are shrinking due to the pet trade, but the Puerto Rican parrot was disappearing due to habitat conversion and deforestation. Before the US and Spain unleashed their avarice upon the small landmass's resources, finding the Puerto Rican parrot would have been a slam dunk. Puerto Rico was its oyster; the strident birds had an abundance of fruit, seeds, and tree cavities for nesting. The population grew to a million-strong, more than enough to withstand the fickle Caribbean tempests that routinely ripped across the island.

But people want lumber. With the trees went the parrots. The population crashed. Conspicuously absent, in 1967, the Puerto Rican parrot—*Amazona vittata*—was listed as federally endangered. Remaining parrots were rounded up, placed in large aviaries, and encouraged to breed. Parrot lovemaking took time. Gradually offspring were released into the surrounding forest. Despite attentive intervention, just thirteen parrots flew about two small forest patches in 1975. They've been on life support ever since, gains in the population offset by recurrent hurricanes. At last count, the number of wild parrots hovered around two hundred.

"Notice that the color of the bird perfectly matches the color of the leaves," I told my class, a photo of the lime green bird next to a map of the country behind me on a screen. "It's simple math: Two hundred is a small number and Puerto Rico is the size of Connecticut. The country's billion-odd leaves outnumber the parrot. And since the canopy happens to be where the parrots hang out, we have no chance. Nada."

"Aww," Anna said, "they're so cute."

My academic training had scrubbed out most mushy words, but Anna was right. Puerto Rican parrots were hopelessly cute. Chunky, large-eyed, and a dollop of red on their forehead gave them a look of having just investigated a ketchup bottle. Puerto Ricans adored them, too; the bird was an unofficial emblem of the island's uniqueness, the avian equivalent of the coqui frog.

"But," I said, changing the slide to a drab bird that looked like a grackle, "we have an excellent shot of seeing this." Their silence spoke loudly. I pressed on. "Behold the yellow-shouldered blackbird!"

"I don't see any yellow," Andrew said from the second row.

"It's like a Siamese fireback," I replied.

"A what?"

"Never mind. What I mean is, the bird can conceal the yellow in its wings whenever it wants," I explained, "like our red-winged black-bird that it's closely related to."

"This bird is endemic?" Emily asked. I sensed her skepticism, academia might serve her well.

"Some consider it a subspecies of the tawny-shouldered blackbird of Cuba," I said, "but most taxonomies separate them."

"What's so special about it?" Ben asked.

"What's special about anything? That's a philosophical question." Ben scowled. "You know what makes it special to me?" I asked. Nobody cared, but I continued anyway. "Because it's rare."

"How rare?"

"Rare enough to be put on the endangered species list."

"What makes you think we'll find it?" Emily asked, again with a hint of skepticism.

"Seagull Steve," I replied. Nobody spoke, but now I had their attention. "I squandered a good hour of my life reading his blog today," I explained. "Seagull Steve has searched for Puerto Rico's endemics and written about it. He said the only place to reliably find them is a locally owned hardware store in La Paguera, a little town on the south-ern coast. To see the blackbird, we'll have to show up a little before three." A sea of quizzical faces met mine. "That's when the owner tosses out unsold bread."

"That's so random."

"Why does a hardware store sell bread?"

"Who calls himself Seagull Steve?"

I shrugged. "A guy with a sense of humor. Let's hope he knows birds as well he knows Hollywood. Great as his blog name is, Steve should know there's no such thing as seagulls. Just gulls."

In El Yunque, Puerto Rico's sole National Forest, there weren't many gulls. But the lovely rainforest park where we kicked off our trip had everything else. As soon as we climbed out of the vans, todies—birds that look like tiny tennis balls—burped out strange, monosyllabic calls from the surrounding vegetation. A curious pearly-eyed thrasher (my chosen name, if I start a blog of my own or ever join a Seattle grunge band) scrambled about. Above, Caribbean martins carved up the airspace.

Sensing I didn't have a plan, my type A students quickly formed one. "Let's go to Mount Britton Tower," Seth said. "Perhaps we'll be able to see black swifts up there!" Seth was the most formidable birder in the group. He had added much needed specifics to my otherwise vague itinerary. He was also one of the University's best track athletes.

The rest of the class were not track athletes. Before long, the group split and the slower group—now lagging far behind—decided to head back. "I'll go ahead with the tower group," I said. "We'll meet you back at the vans at two." I charged on ambitiously, but a bit concerned about the group headed back. They'd be twiddling their thumbs for a few hours.

I needn't have worried. When we reunited back at the vans, they hardly noticed. Most were taking selfies with a slug they'd found, and laughing with a slight, bright-eyed Puerto Rican. "This is Jose!" Kimberlyn said. "He has showed us the coolest snails and mushrooms."

"He even caught us a coqui frog," Anna chimed in. Jose turned to me, smiling ear-to-ear. "Do you want to hold the slug?" The slug was placed on my forearm before I could respond.

"Can we keep him?" Kimberlyn asked, putting her hands together.

"The slug?"

"Jose!" Kimberlyn said.

"Um, I'm pretty sure Jose has somewhere to be," I said.

"But he said he can be our guide," Kimberlyn pleaded. "He knows everything." I looked at Jose.

"Not everything," he corrected. "But I know where you can find a Puerto Rican parrot." These were the magic words.

"You do?" I stared at him.

"Of course. I'm a guide."

"You work here?"

"Of course." Jose's English was superb and—of course—I loved his self-assurance. "But I'm free the next two days. It's my weekend."

"I didn't budget for a guide." But Jose waved me off.

"No need," he said. "I love you guys," he said, motioning at the students. They looked at me beseechingly. I didn't know this man at all, and it probably wasn't wise to invite a stranger on a whim.

"He says he knows where you can see the owl, too!" Kimberlyn interjected. She knew me too well.

"The Puerto Rican screech owl?"

"Of course. Guanica Dry Forest." Jose looked at his watch. "What time should I meet you there tomorrow morning?"

"You'll meet us?" Guanica was almost two hours away. I had arranged many trips in Africa with local guides. Arranged meetings were as likely as high heels on a pig. Perhaps this was another yes culture where politeness demanded promises that people had no intention of keeping. I stifled my skepticism and thrust out my hand. "Eight o'clock at the forest gate?"

"See you there," Jose said. "Kimberlyn has my contact if you get lost."

Kimberlyn, self-appointed shotgun rider, sat next to me as we pulled out of El Yunque. "Isn't Jose great? He taught us so much while you all were gone. Can you believe he's going to be with us the next two days?"

"Don't hold your breath," I muttered. Kimberlyn looked at me, her brow furrowed.

"Wait, you don't think he's going to show up?"

"No chance," I said. "People do this all the time in Tanzania. They can't say no to your face."

"How much you wanna bet?" Kimberlyn challenged.

"I'm your professor. I can't take your money. No way, Jose."

Kimberlyn didn't laugh.

Thankfully, I didn't put money down. The next morning, Jose was waiting for us at the gate. He high-fived the ranger and jogged over.

"I told you!" Kimberlyn shouted joyfully. Dumbfounded, I rolled down the window.

"I should have told you to meet at six." Jose began. "But my friend over there says an owl has been hanging around. Let's go find it!"

Laden with water bottles and besmeared in sunscreen, we hit the trail. Heat radiated from the loose gravel as we made our way up a hillslope. The dry forest was aptly named, leaves looked wilted on the short, skeletonized trees. But the apocalyptic landscape didn't dampen the spirits of an Adelaide's warbler that welcomed us with a bouncy song. Enchanted by the mustard yellow bird, nobody noticed Jose disappear.

"Jose!" Connor called from the back of the line. "Jose? Hey, where'd he go?"

"He was right next to me a minute ago," Ben said.

"Let's look for shade," I said, "lest we perish."

"Without Jose?"

"I'm sure he knows where we are," I said. My earlier skepticism had done a 180. Of course Jose knew where we were—he knew everything. Minutes later, he popped out of the forest well ahead of us. He waved and disappeared again, repeating the routine several more times. Must have a stomach bug, I thought, opting not to inquire.

"Eli, Dave's not doing so good," Andrew said, motioning me over. Dave was slumped over in a sliver of shade, fanning himself. Andrew dribbled water over his head. Only diehard Seth was still birding, binoculars combing the branches. Everybody else was flagging. Some looked wan, upright sausages slowly frying. Birds had gone quiet; even the Adelaide's warbler had gone mute. "I think we need to get Dave back to the van," Andrew said. "Get him some AC."

Jose reappeared, this time behind us. A finger to his lips, he motioned us over and pointed into a thick tangle. "I see it," Connor whisper-shouted. A stone's throw away, in a small shrub, was the Puerto Rican owl. It was fuzzy brown on top and had streaking down its chest. The owl showed little fear as it returned our gaze with black, bottomless eyes. Then something cool: The owl blinked. Its eyelids were as orange as a carrot. Behind the owl, another pair of eyes appeared: Jose's. He had reentered the forest and circled the owl. He flashed two thumbs up and then slowly backed away.

Binoculars weren't needed. Reverential silence enveloped us. All eyes studied the bird. Dave, now standing beside me and smiling, looked better. After a few minutes and a thousand photos, I signaled a retreat. The owl's healing gift was sufficient.

Sufficient indeed. Our feet felt lighter, and Dave opted against an early retreat to the vans. The Guanica Dry Forest had other endemic birds on offer: A woodpecker with a raspberry-stained belly and a lizard-cuckoo that cackled like a hyena. When we eventually returned to the vans, two other cars were in the parking lot. One belonged to serious pair of Spandex-clad mountain bikers, the other to an entomologist from West Virginia. Not typical beach-seeking tourists. They had come to Puerto Rico on separate missions with atypical goals: endorphins, arthropods, and adventure.

Our goal was atypical too, and beach interest had waned. On day one, my students sprinted headlong into the surf, reddened into lobsters, and emptied San Juan of aloe vera. They hadn't pressed me to return. The beach hadn't pushed them away. Rather, birds had pulled them in. Now they preferred bushwhacking to basking. Jose flicked his wand and pulled an owl out of his hat. Deeper magic was at work.

—

Magic can be hard to find when you don't know where—or who—you are. Many of us in the West are de-placed. David Orr writes that, for us, "immediate places are no longer sources of food, water, livelihood, energy, materials, friends, recreation, or sacred inspiration." As such, they become compartmentalized, distinct and aloof from the resources we consume. For educators, Orr concludes, this makes the concept of place harder to understand and communicate—it becomes abstract.

Birds can't afford to be de-placed. If immediate places don't offer the resources they need, they die.

La Parguera's hardware store, which offered everything from saw sharpeners to swimsuits, seems an odd place think about the concept of place. But, evidenced by all the food we purchased, it certainly had resources. I herded my students out the back to a few benches scattered under the deep shade of an old mango tree. A complex of ramshackle feeders surrounded the store's back steps like stalagmites. At precisely three o'clock, the owner, balding and pudgy, tottered out with a wooden tray of unsold bread. La Parguera's birds knew the drill. On cue, an eager flock of greater Antillean grackles—"gags" to us—descended en masse, along with a few adaptable foreigners: Eurasian and African collared doves. Once the initial onslaught passed, the comely star showed up.

"I see one!" Seth said, pointing overhead. A yellow-shouldered blackbird hopped along a large limb, as nondescript as the store itself. Except for the small lemon slice in its wing and a thinner, pointier bill, it was indistinguishable from the garrulous gags. We sat contentedly, humans and birds, stuffing our faces with food, our sense of place—and reliance upon it—more apparent.

It's true, there is no such thing as a seagull. But there is such a thing as late afternoon commensalism with an endemic blackbird at a hardware store. Steve was right on the money.

Commensalism with the Puerto Rican parrot would be a coup, but much harder than the owl and blackbird. Jose needed to go back to work. He made one final promise: Tomorrow morning, before skedaddling, he'd show us the best place to look. After that, success hinged on luck. Jose had been better than his word; even so, I couldn't shake my skepticism. The bird's population was too low, accessibility to its haunts too restricted. "We can see this bird," Jose assured me after we bid the blackbird adieu. "Meet me at the Rio Abajo gate at eight o'clock. The birds are only there in the morning. If you're late, you'll miss them."

We weren't late. But a large gate barred our entry into the national forest. Unsurprisingly, Jose had beat us. He leaned against the gate, one hand resting on the oversized padlock. Several large-lettered no trespassing signs were posted nearby, a red painted skull and crossbones on one. Here, finally, was an obstacle we couldn't get around.

As Jose approached my window, two white pickup trucks pulled up. Had surveillance cameras monitored our arrival? I gulped as two uniformed men stepped out. Jose intercepted them, probably to keep me from foiling his plan. Jose had his back to us. All I saw were the officers' expressions, which revealed little. Finally, one nodded and stuck out his hand. Jose gave it a firm shake and bounded over.

"They're letting us in!" he said, cheerfully. "They won't let us walk the trails but it's fine if we explore the grounds."

"Seriously?" I couldn't believe our luck.

"Of course. Vamos!"

Trails proved unnecessary. The headquarter grounds were drenched in birds. Puerto Rican vireos, flycatchers, orioles, and pewees flitted about. A pair of loggerhead kingbirds exchanged duties at a nest in a snag. Todies ferried insects to their young, hidden away in an unseen burrow. Bird by bird we went, reveling in the antics of each.

Strident screeching pierced our reverie. We looked up. Four pea-green, globular bodies shimmied at the top of a wispy fruit tree, stark against the cobalt sky. A dollop of ketchup marked each forehead, and white rings outlined each pair of eyes. The birds—Puerto Rican parrots—looked as surprised to have company as we did. Dexterously, they tore fruits off the tree, shattered hulls pattering down like rain.

The four birds each claimed a limb, shrieking with each plucked fruit. A million of these could drown out the Caribbean. There could be no midday siesta with these birds around; maybe this was why people cut down the forests. Then, as quickly as it started, the cacophony ceased. The four birds froze, heads cocked, eyes skyward. Two broad-winged hawks cruised overhead. Muzzled with fear, the parrots bolted, their silent bodies deliquescing into the canopy.

I looked at my watch: half-past eight. Had we been much later, or had it taken longer to talk our way onto the grounds, we would have missed the crown jewels.

Even with the parrots, my pessimistic prophecy proved true: We didn't see all of Puerto Rico's endemic birds. The Puerto Rican night-jar proved too elusive even for Jose—but thanks to him, we came within one bird of a clean sweep. My trinity of academic traits—ambition, perseverance, and skepticism—had been tweaked. Anything was possible. Skepticism had disappeared with the parrots.

In its place now perches something greater, something memorable and magical: munificence. It takes form in students striking up a new friendship, Seagull Steve's detailed blog, a thoughtful hardware store, compassionate forest officials, and a punctual guide who understands place. All are required to glimpse the carrot-colored eyelids of an owl. The lemon slice on a blackbird's shoulders. The dollop of ketchup on an endangered parrot.

Deracinate

Uproot (someone) from their natural geographical, social, or cultural environment.

Tawny Frogmouth

Bird names are important. They can reveal lineage, convey identity, and point to important field marks. Bird names can also hurt, depending on whom the innocent birds are named after. Plenty of names have changed since I spied my first chestnut-sided warbler, and many more are sure to follow. Nomenclature, like a species, is in perpetual flux. Change is to be expected: molecular techniques advance, taxonomies improve, and our cultural sensibilities get refined. I accept it like my hair loss: inevitable and—hopefully—a signpost of greater wisdom.

But some names, so help me, better not change. Ever. They're too evocative, too multi-syllabic, or too hard to say without laughing out loud. Just think: A fluffy-backed tit-babbler pokes through moist lowland forests of Southeast Asia. A yellow-rumped tinkerbird bops about East Africa thornscrub. A brown creeper lurks around my house in western New York. Enough said.

Fault can surely, by someone, be found with these names. But delight, too. King of Saxony bird-of-paradise, pyrrhuloxia, superb fairywren: These names have pushed me to Wikipedia, spell check, and mystical worlds, sometimes all at once. Yellow-bellied sapsucker remains my mentally bookmarked, fifth-grade comeback. Other names—American woodcock, horned screamer—are bookmarked for a different reason: never to utter in mixed company. Then there's the smew. I've never seen a smew. But if I do, I'll wrinkle my nose as if someone near me passed gas and say: A smew. Ew!

More than a few are as good as smew. I relish them. The way they rattle around my mouth and my—too often puerile—imagination. They make me long for the chase, to decide for myself whether the appellation is apt. Is the monotonous lark truly longwinded? Does the tinkling cisticola use a restroom? Should an exorcism be performed on the satanic nightjar? Does a sandwich tern ham it up? Long-tailed hermit that I am, I comb the internet for flamboyant names. I flip through field guides. Birds and words are my tonic. I muse and muse. Me, the bald-spotted muser.

Another trinity: Musing, pedagogy, and Zugunruhe. Mixed, the alchemy can stir imagination—and migration. This past spring, it led to ten days of itinerant teaching in New Zealand, a trip that, with some shrewd scheduling, allowed me thirty-six jetlagged hours to investigate the oddly named birds of Melbourne, Australia. Is a buff-rumped thornbill's rump buffy? Do white-plumed honeyeaters slurp up honey? Is a noisy miner cacophonous? Luck, coupled with caffeine, might give me answers. Overshadowing all was a bird whose name stirred my imagination more than any other: the tawny frogmouth.

Like the smew, I was a frogmouth fan from books alone. One book actually. Simply titled *Tawny Frogmouth*, it had jumped into my hands at a used book sale under a musty awning at my town's annual blueberry festival. The lack of a subtitle suggested that the no nonsense author lacked creativity to come up with one. Or, that the tawny frogmouth was spellbinding enough to make it unnecessary. I assumed the latter, forked over a dollar and made off with my prize.

It turned out to be both. The author, Gisela Kaplan, had spent a decade studying the bird and shoehorned every possible frogmouth fact into her technical treatise. Australia seemed to have a corner on endemism, a concept that had become central to my own search for place. A whopping 46 percent of the continent's birds were endemic, meaning they're unique and that they've been true to their place of origin. In part, the frogmouth is loyal to place because it's a branch potato. Kaplan, more generous, calls it "remarkably sedentary." However you characterize it, frogmouths don't fly if they don't have to. A pair may defend a sixty-acre territory, though another source says three acres are sufficient for some.

All they need are three basic requirements: a decent food supply, roosting sites, and a place to build a nest. The same things, in other words, we all need. If these are in place, frogmouths will never leave. Site fidelity—oxymoronically—in action. One dedicated researcher observed a pair remain on the same dinky patch of territory for six years. When the female's partner died, she stayed put until another male finally moved in. If you've got a good thing going, stay put. If the bottom falls out, stay put even longer. But, for the frogmouth lineage to continue, somebody—at some point—has to move.

In the introduction, Kaplan couldn't help but break away from factual prose in defense of the frogmouth's appearance. "In a recent magazine story," she wrote, "it was even claimed that the prize of the world's most unfortunate-looking bird must surely go to that golden-eyed, lock-jawed frogmouth." Though she didn't explain, she planted her flag. "The connotation of 'frogmouth' seems thoroughly undeserved in my opinion." I was intrigued. Here was a scientist slipping out of science-speak to offer a plainspoken objection to what most considered a trivial common name; intrigued, yes, but not enough to finish. Bogged down in chapter two, I slipped the book onto a shelf where it remained, like the bird, remarkably sedentary.

I wished I had finished it. Upon landing at Melbourne's Tullamarine Airport, I had no idea what habitat the frogmouth preferred, nor what its habits were. Too cheap to pay for a rental, I stashed my suitcase in a storage locker and hailed a cab. Full of frugality, false-confidence and frogmouth zeal, I opted against a SIM card for my phone. Fifteen minutes later, I hopped out at Woodlands Historic Park, a seven-hundred-hectare preserve. I asked Nick, my edgy, slick-haired driver to pick me back up at three o'clock that afternoon.

"Just call me," he said, handing me his card.

"I can't."

"Why?"

"No service," I said, pointing to my phone. Nick furrowed his brow.

"Pick you up where?"

"Here." Nick looked out his window and frowned.

"I'll do my best, mate." Before I could respond, his phone rang. "Gotta go," he said. "Cheers."

"Cheers," I replied sourly, watching his taillights grow smaller. How good was Nick's site fidelity? I looked around, scanning for landmarks. The only notable feature appeared to be some kind of garden store down the road. Garden store with yellow sign, I repeated to myself. Be here by three. Nick's livelihood depended on customers like me. He would show up. Munificence couldn't be limited to Puerto Rico.

Doubt melted away as soon as I wandered into the park. Eyes wide, I was a kid in a candy store. I looked at my watch. Ten a.m. That gave me four hours to find a frogmouth, one hour to find Nick. No sweat.

No sweat indeed, the chilly, autumn air made me cinch down my hood. No matter, operation frogmouth was underway. But here, I was a hapless house sparrow, drawn in by Australia's retinue of novelty. Every bird was new. My first was dusty and drab. I studied it, lowered my binoculars, and found a match on page 116 of my field guide. Buff-rumped thornbill. The rump did look buffy, the bill thorny. Check. One point to the naming committee.

Pockets full and shoulder bag too crammed with snacks, I jammed my field guide into the back of my pants. Awkward. Uncomfortable. But if I fell backward onto an echidna, I'd live to tell the tale.

Hoo-hoo-hoo-hoo-hoo-ha-ha-ha-ha-ha-ha-ha-ha-ha-ha!

Ah ha! I knew this sound. I'd played it to wake up sleepy classes in the states. I crept forward toward a stand of eucalyptus. On a sweeping, horizontal branch was a laughing kookaburra, a name derived from an onomatopoeic loanword from the Indigenous Wiradjuri: guuguubarra. The huge, terrestrially minded kingfisher sported an ebony eyeline, flecks of turquoise in its wings, and a bill that looked perfect for cleaning out my shower drain. Compared to the thornbill, the kookaburra's thick neck and stout frame made it look like an Olympic powerlifter. After a prolonged crescendo, the maniacal laughter mercifully ceased. And I thought Puerto Rican parrots were bad. Another well named bird. Check.

Kookaburra, red wattlebird, two dozen rainbow lorikeets. One bird led me to another until out of nowhere, I was mobbed by a surly group of bouncers—kangaroos. It's uncertain who was more wary, me or the mob. Upright, yes, but maybe not their intentions. After a prolonged stare-down, they pogoed off.

A buzz-plink-plink rising out of the grass kept me from ruing (ahem) their departure. Another half-dozen footsteps kicked up a golden-headed cisticola. Bathed in sunshine, maybe the head shined like gold; on this overcast afternoon, it was decidedly cinnamon and limited only to the crown. The rest of the bird was earthy, with dirty gray grease marks around the eyes. The naming committee paid this fellow a favor. Less charitably, and more accurately, the golden-headed cisticola could have been called the smudge-faced buzzhead.

I scrambled down a ravine, edged around a pond, and entered a vast grove of eucalyptus. For a park so near the airport, the lack of people in this ecological wonderland was odd. Perhaps it was the pitiless weather. I glanced at my watch. 2:00 p.m. I had wandered for four hours without a bite of food. Nor considered an exit strategy. Frogmouth or not, it was time to head back to my rendezvous point and wait for Nick.

Unsure where to go, I climbed up a nearby promontory. My destination, Melbourne, arose in the east, its buildings like distant dominoes in the misting rain. Where had I started from? Trees cluttered the foreground. I chose south and started walking. I'd been lucky so far.

Maybe my luck would hold.

It didn't. An hour passed and nothing looked familiar. I hadn't even managed to find a park boundary or road. Halfway across a field, a tattooed guy with earbuds was walking a squat, short-snouted dog. Eager for something to attack, the toothy dog spied me and towed its reluctant owner over. I maintained a healthy distance, lest it rip my legs off. "Is there a garden store around here?" I asked. The guy pulled out an earbud.

"Sorry?"

"Uh, I'm looking for a garden store," I repeated.

"Would love to help mate, but just moved in myself." Saliva drool fell off his dog's flat face.

"Well, can you at least tell me how to get out of here?"

"The park?" He looked at me like the idiot that I was. "Well, where you'd come in from?"

"That's the problem. I'm not sure." He cast me a look of pity. His dog one of menace.

"Uh… Just follow this path," he said, motioning behind him. "It'll take you to Somerton Road. Take Somerton to Greenvale. Maybe your garden store is there?"

"Thanks," I said, eager to put some distance between me and his muderous pet.

"Doubt much will be open with Easter and all," he added, reinserting his earbud. No matter. All I needed was a gas station and a bit of Aussie benevolence. Without any other leads, and well past my three o'clock meetup with Nick, I powerwalked down the path.

Heavy legs and disorientation didn't quell the birds, or my tendency to notice them. A loose flock of white-breasted woodswallows slowed my progress. Like most of the day's creatures, the woodswallows busted my tidy bird categories. Some sat contentedly on limbs while others soared, pointed wings slicing the sky. In the passerine world, comprising half the world's perching birds, soaring is a rare feat most often reserved for longer winged raptors and seabirds. When the woodswallows weren't chasing insects on the wing, they could drop onto flowers and slurp up nectar with bifurcated tongues, another rare trait in the bird world. White breasts, check. In and around woods, check. Swallow-like, check. Well done, naming committee.

Somerton Road brought instant—and discomfiting—relief. While it assured me that my toes wouldn't be nibbled by eastern barred bandicoots come nightfall, it underscored absolute dependence upon my fellow species. I had become lost in a suburban park. Rugged survivalist I wasn't. Tail between my legs, I headed east and wound through a ritzy development with small shops, all shuttered for Easter. By four o'clock, I still hadn't found a gas station or anything that was open. My food was almost gone. I took inventory: One granola bar, two swallows of water, a dead phone, and luggage fifteen miles away in the Melbourne Airport. I did have matches. Maybe I could light a fire with the pages from my field guide. Still stored in the back of my pants, at least it was dry. Or, of course, I could hitchhike. Do people hitchhike in Australia?

Back in my twenties, when I had eagerly hitchhiked part of Hawaii to see honeycreepers; the act felt like a rite of passage. Twenty-five years later, wet, jetlagged, and hopelessly deracinated, I hesitated. This was the reason species stayed put. Knowledge of landmarks, directions, and neighbors—having ready access to resources—was comforting, and survival depended on it. Travel is cool, but for crying out loud, loosen the purse strings and buy a SIM card. Or, like the frogmouth, stay put. My dark mood matched the sky.

Street lights flickered on. I forged ahead and cut through a vacant parking lot, scanning for signs of humanity. A nondescript strip mall offered cosmetic surgery, health foods, and at the end, Roo Hair and Beauty. I headed for the salon, mostly because of the glorious, four-letter word that glowed red beneath it: "open."

Tentatively, I stepped inside, triggering an electronic beep. Four unoccupied salon chairs were fixed to the waxed, shiny floor, and surrounded by spotlessly clean mirrors. Momentarily I was alone. A woman stepped into the salon wearing a saffron sari and a nervous smile. I guessed her thoughts: If only she'd locked the door a moment before. I caught site of myself in the mirror. Yikes! Wet and haggard, dark circles enshrouded my bloodshot eyes. "This is going to sound really stupid," I blurted, smiling to reassure her that I hadn't arrived to make off with an armload of sulfate-free shampoos and bonding conditioners. "I'm trying to get to the airport and my phone is dead." I neglected to add that my brain was dead, too.

"Let me call my son," she said, scurrying through a door. Seconds later, a trim, thirty-something man emerged flanked by what appeared to be another son and maybe her husband, the latter of whom had a white beard that was cinched at the bottom. Two waist-high children eyed me bashfully.

"What's up?" said the son with none of his mother's caution. As I explained, he handed me his phone and motioned me to sit in the styling chair. It felt like a throne.

"Some tea?" the husband asked, bowing slightly and clasping his hands. Their personal story tumbled out. The family had recently immigrated from Sri Lanka. Though they missed their birthplace, they uprooted for opportunity. Now they were carving out a pleasant, albeit culturally lonely, life outside Melbourne. They marveled when I told them I was from New York. I shattered their misapprehension that I was from the iconic city when I let it slide that I lived in one of the most underpopulated counties in the state. Fifteen minutes later, a taxi pulled up. Not wanting to impose, I refused tea, biscuits, and hair treatment, though I certainly could have used all three. Grateful, I eased out of the ergonomic chair, thanked them profusely, and headed out the door.

"Come anytime!" the mother called after me, now smiling, as I got in the cab. Confident I wouldn't, her relief was palpable. More benevolence at the hands of perfect strangers; at least I had given them something to talk about. I headed back to the airport, struck by the fact that my rescue came in an Australian beauty salon run by Sri Lankan immigrants. Had they not relocated to that particular suburb, I might have passed a hungry night curled up outside a health foods store. Migration is a complicated affair.

Sometime later, I wheeled my luggage into the YHM Hostel in downtown Melbourne. Head full of birds and bone tired, I wolfed down a plate of pasta, took a long overdue shower, and collapsed atop a bunk in a men's dorm. None of the other bunks were occupied. A blessed night of sleep awaited.

A blessed hour, rather. If you desire a memorably horrid night, spend it in a room full of itinerant, somnolent, tourists who have drunk one too many Victoria bitters. The shadowy room now resembled a homeless shelter. Belongings were strewn about and blanketed occupants lined the room, inhaling air like warthogs and exhaling it like spouting whales. I pulled on headphones, blasted Def Leppard, and willed myself back to—now fitful—sleep.

At dawn, warthog and whale symphony still raging, I ripped out of the hostile hostel, hopeful that the shoes I slipped on in the dark were my own. Morning traffic never sounded so lovely—as did the prospect of roaming Melbourne to search for birds. Humbled by the previous evening and unwilling to chance my late afternoon flight to my internal compass, I limited my frogmouth quest to the city confines. While more time would have been ideal, finite time to search adrenalized me. Using the creased map I'd picked up at the hostel, I turned right on the St. Kilda Street Bridge.

Midway, dozens of little corellas arced overhead, the pearly white flock resembling a snow squall over the Yarra River's indigo water. One lit upon a streetlight and looked down at me, a blush of magenta dappled on its forehead. This was the sulfur-crested cockatiel's smaller, comelier sister; pretty enough to share a plate with the cockatiel in my field guide, but not enough to slow the stream of pedestrians and bicyclists that swerved around me. Crow-sized, "little" didn't seem to fit. But little corella had a nice ring, surely better than "tomato-faced hookbill" or "bleached-out blue-eye," that less charitable committees could have come up with.

I swung left, ascended a hill, and walked through an open iron gate, signifying I was now in the Royal Botanic Gardens. Botanic gardens are godsends for time-strapped bird lovers. Little islands of refuge, they offer shade, shelter, water, and often, a bevy of nectar-rich blossoms. Royal sounds as well, bell miners heralded my passage, chiming across the manicured lawns. Silvereyes, scrub-wrens, and spinebills flitted about the foliage as I flitted about my field guide, eager to identify them. Vegetated ponds revealed a nankeen night heron, silver gulls, purple swamphens, black swans, and an Australasian darter that I initially mistook for a misplaced African finfoot. If only.

The hours leaked away; I was a hostage of time. Just two hours remained until I had to be at the airport. For my date with the frogmouth, it was now or never.

Two options remained: I could comb the hundreds of dense, leafy trees for an immobile, cryptically patterned bird; or I could seek intel. The first option depended on dumb luck, and I had used up my allotment at the Sri Lankan beauty bar. That left option two.

I made for the visitor center and walked up to the counter. "I have a weird question," I asked a woman with long auburn hair that cascaded out the back of a green, full-brimmed hat.

"We get lots of those. Fire away."

"I'm looking for a tawny frogmouth."

"A what?" she said, screwing up her face.

"A tawny frogmouth," I repeated.

"What is that?" Rats—her lack of comprehension wasn't a good sign.

"A cool bird," I said. "Kind of like an owl."

"Afraid not," she said. Seeing my face fall, she added, "But we do have a checklist of the garden's birds, if you're interested." I wasn't. Ebird had assured me the frogmouth was here. I didn't need a checklist to confirm it.

"Well, thanks anyway," turning toward the door.

"Did I hear you say you were looking for a frogmouth?" a voice called out from an open door behind the counter. I spun around. A dark-featured kid, who hardly looked to be out of university, emerged. He wore a similar flat-brimmed hat. "Go to Oak Lawn. Off the path, amid the larger trees, you'll find a skinny Guadeloupe Island Oak. It's labeled. A pair of frogmouths roost in it, but I haven't heard any recent reports."

With a nod, I rocketed out the door.

A birder's life is often tip-based. You give and receive, eager for others to enjoy the same special bird—the same special moment—that you did. I've received tips to specific locations, but this was the first to a specific tree—extreme site fidelity. At Oak Lawn, I beelined from tree to tree, handy labels telling me which oak was which. The Guadeloupe Island Oak was hardly larger than a flagpole, the kind of tree loggers wouldn't bother with. Small and scraggily, it was the least impressive in the grove. I walked up to it, my eyes crawling up the trunk. On the third branch from the base was an unmistakable upright lump of feathers. Two yellow eyes leered down at me. One branch further up, four feet out from the trunk, was another. Tawny frogmouths. Avian rhapsody.

"The crucial first step to survival in all organisms is habitat selection," the great biologist E. O. Wilson wrote. "If you get to the right place, everything else is likely to be easier." Perhaps in a world as rich as the Royal Botanic Gardens, this small, scraggily tree was sufficient. Perhaps in western New York, my small, scraggily perch was too.

What wasn't sufficient was Gisela Kaplan's ire for the frogmouth's name. Having finally seen the bird for myself, when I returned home from down under, I pulled Kaplan's book off the shelf. I knew she loathed the bird's common name. What did she feel about its Latin one—*Podargus strigoides*? Her prose said it plainly: "*Podargus* is Latin for 'gouty old man' while strigoides means 'owl-like.'" So, Kaplan concluded, "the tawny frogmouth was introduced to the Australian public as grotesque, ugly, weak-footed, and altogether stupid and silly."

If you have to pick a side, pick Kaplan's. She's an emeritus professor in Animal Behavior at the University of New England and an Honorary Professor at the Queensland Brain Institute. She has authored over 250 research articles, twenty-one books, and holds two PhDs. Yet humbly, I disagree. I love the frogmouth's name. The two birds manifested amphibian likeness: The entirety of the ten minutes I spent staring up at them, neither flinched. Their bulbous eyes and wide mouths were certainly froglike.

But my dissent hinges on a deeper reason. Undeserved or not, the name—tawny frogmouth—hopped into my imagination and stuck. The name and the bird needn't move. They move me. The ceaseless flight of my imagination, and my blitzkrieg through Melbourne, is testament to that.

Fragmentation

The process or state of breaking or being broke into small or separate parts.

American Goshawk

B irding has a code. It's neither secret nor surprising. Many niche hobbies have esoteric shorthand taken for granted by the cognoscenti and ignored or unknown by the casual. Naysayers poopoo the code for good reason, it can marginalize and alienate those who don't know it. As Captain Hector Barbossa would say, "you must be a pirate for the pirate's code to apply and you're not." Plus, like all bird nomenclature, it changes; perfectly good, memorable code tossed asunder as birds get reclassified. The code, in short, can be a barrier to communication. To fully appreciate it, you have to be an exacting sort, which many top birders naturally are.

I am neither exacting, nor a top birder. I don't love change and am pro-communication. Birding, I firmly believe, should be as inclusive possible. All reasons that make me a hypocrite. Because good golly gosh do I love the code. If I had eight more children, I'd name them: Rosa, Hugo, Will, Levi, Lara, Cate, Caty, and Greg.

To a birder, these names are the farthest things from arbitrary. They represent birds, and cool ones at that: Rosa (rock sandpiper) Hugo (Hudsonian godwit), Will (willet), Levi (lesser violetear), Lara (Laysan rail), Cate (Caspian tern), Caty (cattle tyrant), and Greg (great egret). It doesn't take an ornithologist to realize that all these names are four letters long, the same number as the banding codes that were first published by the Bird Banding Laboratory in 1978. Twenty-five years later, the Institute for Bird Populations tweaked them for the sake of inclusivity. Not to include more people, of course; to include more birds.

It goes like this: For one-word bird names, like the mallard, the code is the first four letters, MALL. For two-word birds, like the American robin, it's the first two letters of the first word and the first two of the second: AMRO. For three-word hyphenated names, like the blue-winged teal, it's the first letter of the first word, the first letter of the hyphenated word, and the first two letters of the third word, BWTE. There are other rules for four lettered birds, and scientific names, and blah, blah, blah. If you've exhausted every other remedy for insomnia, a sixteen-page paper, titled "Four-letter and Six-letter Alpha Codes for Birds Recorded from the American Ornithologists' Union Check-list Area," might just do the trick. In it, the authors painstakingly reveal the rules, which are not (as captain Barbossa suggests) mere guidelines. At the risk of you lobbing four-letter words for me, there's a bit more.

Code rules get dicey when two birds collide—not into a window or each other, but in their nomenclature. There are plenty of birds to illustrate this. But only one bird manifests collision in all its murderous glory: the American goshawk. If you started with a peregrine falcon, slowed it down, beefed it up, made it perpetually grouchy, and forced it to live in a forest, you'd have an American goshawk. It's like a raptor that is stuck in traffic and spilled its coffee on its lap. Beware of making eye contact with this bird. "If you want a well-behaved goshawk, you just have to do one thing," Helen Macdonald writes in *H is for Hawk*. "Give 'em the opportunity to kill things. Kill as much as possible. Murder sorts them out."

I fruitlessly searched out this killing machine for three decades. I went to their breeding grounds in spring. I swung over fallen logs. I ripped through raspberry tangles. I scrutinized every raptor that sliced or soared overhead. I found plenty of Cooper's and sharp-shinned hawks, the goshawk's smaller siblings. But never a goshawk. As with Australia's frogmouth, I needed intel, an ace-in-the-hole. So I consulted a secret-sharing oracle, a friend who had spent a summer monitoring their scant breeding locations across Pennsylvania.

"Walk along Forest Road 259. It's an unmarked logging road," Elise confided, including a rudimentary map of the Allegheny National Forest. "We've found goshawks in this section." Wonderful, I thought, the perfect treasure hunt: likely, but not guaranteed. To lay eyes on a goshawk, I'd need wits to augment these vague instructions.

Other than an ominously red check engine light, my prospects seemed good. It was June, nesting should be well underway. This meant the goshawks would be rightfully pugilistic, ready to divebomb anything—or anybody—that came too close. I had been divebombed by other raptors before and had my nose bloodied by a black kite talon in Tanzania. If I found a nest, I wouldn't approach closely, just enough for my binoculars to capture the fine barring down the front, the dark crown, and those menacing, okra eyes. That would do it.

The rutted road narrowed and the trees pressed in, suffocating the evening light. Lichen-encrusted boulders and a rusty, long-abandoned road grader lay along the roadside, dwarfing my old Subaru. I had everything I needed for an overnight in the forest, but if my engine issue got worse, the lack of phone service and this cattle trail of a road wasn't a lovely combination. Fear and joy, an adrenaline-rich cocktail I've grown to savor, tightened my grip on the wheel as I inched along, looking for a level spot to pitch a tent.

In short, goshawk fever outweighed niggling doubt. I had to be here; decades of searching had proven the bird would never come to me. Most of my goshawk searches had occurred in little patches, carved up places that resulted from what ecologists refer to as habitat fragmentation. Goshawks, like spotted owls out west, prefer contiguous forest, mature trees with at least a 60 percent closed canopy.

Allegheny National Forest, comprising over half a million acres—half the size of Rhode Island—had a closed canopy. At least I thought it did. The Cornell Lab described the bird as "widespread but uncommon," with some 92,000 sneaking about America's forests. Compared to 320 million robins that hopped over our lawns, the goshawk was the not-so-proverbial raptor in the treestack.

But the treestack had just gotten a lot smaller—I had a tip. The birds had bred along this road last year. Like the frogmouth, site fidelity should lure them back. Not to the same branch, but maybe the same square mile. This trip had all the ingredients for a memorable encounter and a lovely new bird—and code—to bandy about. Sadly, it also had all the ingredients for the Dunning-Kruger effect.

The Dunning-Kruger effect is a cognitive bias that leads us to overestimate our expertise or abilities in a field in which we distinctly lack it. It's based upon the idea that we lack enough knowledge to realize we don't have enough knowledge. Naturally, it's far easier to see it in other people than recognizing it in ourselves. My past successes finding birds were often based on familiarity I'd built up over previous years. I'd research a bird's habitat, zero in on seasonality, look for clues, and find the bird. Or, a friend would text a recent sighting or tip. Ebird expanded my "friends" and made it easier. I knew the goshawk's habitat. Forest Road 259 was its locality. Sure, I lacked the specific nest tree. But I grew up in Pennsylvania, not Puerto Rico. This was my turf, a slam dunk. Yes way, Jose.

Perched opposite of Dunning-Kruger is humility, a trait far easier to find in the Allegheny National Forest's half million acres than a goshawk.

Humility, of course, is a byproduct of failure. That night, stretched out on my sleeping bag under a canopy of oaks (more than 60 percent closed, mind you), failure was far from my mind. In the morning, I would sniff one out.

What I sniffed, however, was gas. And no, not my own. Acrid

fumes of petroleum seeped up my nostrils and lolled about in my sinus cavities. How could this be? I was in a pristine place, a national forest. The rutted road was little used. I rolled over hoping a change in position would lessen the clingy stench. It didn't. I zipped up my tent's mesh screens and buried my face in my wadded-up cargo pants. But that only combined petroleum with body odor. The rankling odor hounded me like a dementor, permeating everything. I had a choice: risk navigating out of the wooded labyrinth in the dark, or gas myself silly. I elected for the gas. Mercifully, sometime later I slipped into an exhausted, lightheaded delirium.

Only in Melbourne's snore-heavy hostel was I more excited to greet the blue liminal light of dawn. Never mind my dull headache, I was alive! One instant mug of coffee later, I was off, eager to check a goshawk off and escape the gas chamber. I didn't get far. A REVI—a red-eyed vireo—hopped down a beech branch one eye cocked toward a half-built nest in a spindly fork. It fussed about and then sped off. Goshawks could wait, I had never watched a REVI build a nest before. I sat down.

A minute later the vireo returned. Oddly, it hadn't brought any nest lining. Then I realized why. It was building somewhere else. It hopped to the nest, peered inside, and yanked out some material. It repeated this several times until it had a bill full of filigree fibers. I pulled out my journal. Four times the vireo returned and made off with more materials, the nest growing nattier each time. Decades of bird watching and yet here was a novel observation: petite larceny.

When I took leave of the pilfering vireo, A belligerent DEJU — dark-eyed junco—blocked my path. The bird protested my presence, eight grams of chippy, wing-flicking ire. Understanding the code, I sat down on a stump for one of my favorite spring past times: I-Spy. Satisfied I was an unthreatening neanderthal with bedhead, the little gray bird regained its composure, made a few low, darting flights, scampered several yards, and disappeared into a roadcut.

Eyes trained on the spot, I stood, walked slowly forward, and teased apart a curtain of ferns. Shocked by my impropriety, the junco urgently exited stage left to reveal a dainty, grass-woven cup with four pale eggs tucked symmetrically inside. Faint beige freckles dotted each egg's blunter end. Lest the hysterical junco pop a blood vessel, I let the ferns fall back over the abode, jotted down a few more notes, and ambled off. Sacred acts surrounded me. Was this how Saint Francis felt?

Lingering fumes reminded me this was Allegheny, not Assisi. While the national forest offered the quiescence of a monastic retreat, it was anything but. The map showed the forest as a green, amoeba-shaped polygon that stood out from the cluttered squiggles of civilization—Pittsburg, Jamestown, Warren—that surrounded it. This wasn't a national park, managed by a preservation-minded park service. It was managed by a different service—the National Forest Service—a division of the Department of Agriculture. A key distinction: Like crop fields, our nation's 150-plus national forests were never intended to sit idle. Natural resource extraction is permitted. As the first person to lead the US Forest Service, Gifford Pinchot made clear that the nation's forests were "to provide the greatest amount of good for the greatest amount of people in the long run."

"Good" is, of course, in the eyes of the beholder. Pinchot's didn't extend to good for goshawks. Like all raptors, goshawks were viewed as our competitors in Pinchot's time, hence why they were conspicuously not included among the species protected by one of America's first counts of conservation legislation, the Migratory Bird Treaty Act of 1918. The motto of the National Forest Service remains: "Caring for the land and serving people." Serving people, I begrudgingly realized, included weekend ATV rallies.

The first vehicle sounded like a hungry, hippo-sized mosquito. Saint Francis certainly didn't have to contend with these, I frowned. Reason for optimism remained. In the gigantic miasma of forking roads and nameless tracks, chances were good the wheeled beast wouldn't come my way. But the sounds intensified and soon became a growing, pitchy symphony. The lone mosquito became a cloud. Invasion whined my way.

Grumpily, I stomped off the trail and sat down on a moss-covered log. The parade arrived. Deafened and with nothing better to do, I counted them. One, two, three ... twenty-two, twenty-three, twenty-four... Thirty-three hell-raising, music-blasting, dirt-throwing ATVs and side-by-sides careened by, each coating the one behind it with dust. Each mini-monster truck was full of yeehawing, beverage-holding passengers. I had come to list birds. Instead, I listed the testosterone-infused quad names: Renegade, Zforce, Kingquad, Scrambler. The last one hurt: Raptor.

I sat a bus-length away in full view. Nobody saw me or even looked my way. They were going too fast, too intent on avoiding collisions to risk a sideways glance. Here in this remarkably rich tapestry, the rally-goers saw nothing but the dirty taillights of the machine in front of them. I was invisible. As was the vireo and junco, the latter of which likely suffered a heart attack from 128 wheels ripping past its home.

It did look fun, at least for the lead vehicle. My hypocrisy was evident: I had myself driven in, equally implicated in fossil fuel dependence and ecosystem disruption. Edward Abbey recognized our collective guilt and offered a solution. "Let the people walk," he wrote in *Desert Solitaire*. "Or ride horses, bicycles, mules, wild pigs—anything—but keep the automobiles and the motorcycles and all their motorized relatives out." Abbey's wrath, of course, was directed toward the use of the national parks, not the national forests. Even so, sitting in a pungent cloud of exhaust-riddled dust, his fix didn't seem so bad.

Desert Solitaire wasn't the first American environmental jeremiad. Nearly one hundred years earlier, George Perkins Marsh published *Man and Nature: Or, Physical Geography as Modified by Human Action*. "Man pursues his victims with reckless destructiveness," Marsh wrote. "[He] has ruthlessly warred on all the tribes of all animated nature whose spoil he could convert to his own uses. Greed is the semi-barbarism of modern times."

Modern times for Marsh was 1864. The Industrial Revolution had yet to flex it rapacious muscles. Bison still teemed across the plains in the millions, though they would soon be hunted to near extinction. (Fewer than 100 would remain by the late 1880s.) Ivory-billed woodpeckers ratcheted up trees in the southern bottomland forests, and passenger pigeons still darkened the skies when they passed overhead. Marsh was a prescient naturalist who saw things for what they were. Then, he extrapolated the data. The economic trendline looked rosy, the ecological one not so much.

The whine slowly died away. I remained immobilized on the log. Judging from the forest's now blanketing silence, I noticed my fellow creatures were too. As the dust settled (literally), the reality was clear: Seeing a goshawk was no go. The irony hurt. NOGO had long been the northern goshawk's shorthand code, until the American Ornithologists' Union split the Northern Goshawk into two species in 2023: the Eurasian goshawk, EUGO, and the American goshawk, AGOS.

AGOS? Shouldn't American Goshawk be AMGO? Yes, but this is the unfortunate reality of a system predicated on priority. AMGO was already claimed by the American goldfinch. Somehow, both species lost out: The American goshawk became AGOS and the American goldfinch became AGOL. Unless you're a bird bander—or well off the deep end—this doesn't matter. What does matter is how we treat our public lands. Before I left Allegheny National Forest, I got another whiff.

Back on my feet, I rejoined Forest Road 259, hung right at a fork and walked until the road dissolved into an indistinguishable trail. There, the source of the night's petroleum fumes revealed itself: A twelve-foot tall pumpjack stood at the path's end, its acute angles in stark contrast with the sinewy saplings around it. Fresh grease on the pumpjack's arms bore witness to recent use. Discarded pipes, gas cans, and rusty, discarded parts peeked out of the surrounding leaves.

Three more times, I rejoined Forest Road 259 and took a side trail, and each time, I arrived at a similar-looking pumpjack slick with petroleum. But the fourth time I left the road, the path didn't peter out. Rather, it swelled and spat me into a vast clearing. Stumps and two-story high log piles pockmarked the shredded earth. With a canopy cover of 5 or 10 percent, sunlight poured in; the forest floor, compacted by logging trucks, was dry and dusty. The goshawk forest had gotten an extreme makeover. Brontosaurus-sized machines sat amid the piles, each looking like the battered survivor of a demolition derby.

Unable to resist, I climbed up the ladder of one machine with a car-sized lobster claw on one end. Door ajar, I slid into the cockpit and sat on the rodent-chewed seat. Crushed energy drink cans and empty Skoal containers rested amid a half inch of sawdust on the floor. Out the cracked windshield, I noticed orange surveyor tape wrapped around several of the largest—still upright—trees. Marked for harvest. At the clearing's edge, they looked exposed and vulnerable, a line of dominoes edging a busy sidewalk. As I stared, a RBWO—red-bellied woodpecker—hitched up the nearest and disappeared. A nest hole.

Yesterday, I had driven past a big, brown sign proclaiming Allegheny National Forest, along with a pithy descriptive phrase: "Land of Many Uses." The Forest Service could not be accused of false advertising; it never claimed "wise use." This, too, was a code.

I walked back to my campsite, thoughts careening into one another. Was this what Pinchot had in mind? The greatest good for the greatest number for the longest time? Or was it a manifestation of the Dunning-Kruger Effect writ large, a grand overestimation of our collective expertise?

I'm an ecologist, spared by academia from difficult decisions and impossible trade-offs. Managing our national forests is a country-sized balancing act. My analyses are limited to the knowledge I absorb from technical papers, first-hand observation, and gut feelings. What can I do? Hunt for goshawks, confess my complicity, admit the limitations of my knowledge, and ask questions.

How can we use our forests better? What are the best uses? How should we extract? How much do we really need? How important are goshawks?

I will always continue to question our land use, but I'll never question the bird code. Here's why. I never went looking for it. The code found me—and eventually an AGOS did too. As for the code, friends just started tossing it around, my bird chats and emails filling up with mysterious references to BTGW, TUTI, and MODO sightings. Too sheepish to reveal my ignorance, I sleuthed out the meaning and smiled every time one happened to spell a word. What could be better than spying COME (common merganser) HOME (hooded merganser) on my way back from work? Or watching a KILL (killdeer) on a Saturday afternoon?

The American goshawk found me more dramatically. It sliced through a stand of maples and made for my head. Instinctively, I fell to the ground and covered my neck as a second goshawk deafened the forest with an ear-splitting KEK-KEK-KEK-KEK-KEK from a nearby white pine. I stood up, binned the bird, and rattled off the field marks: fine barring down the front, dark crown, menacing okra eyes. American goshawk: my very first AGOS. Found, not surprisingly, several states away in a differently protected, more intact forest.

NOGO is a better code. I could question the American Ornithologists' Union and petition the Institute for Bird Populations to have AGOS changed back to NOGO. But I'm confident the Institute would be disinclined to acquiesce to my request. If such jargon rankles by this point and you're just a humble reader, it means no. Thanks Captain Barbossa.

Tonypandy

*A falsified version of history
that supplants the facts
in the public consciousness.
Once established, Tonypandy
can be hard to displace.*

EURASIAN COOT

Nobody cares about coots.

When you're on a bicycle, though, you begin to care about a lot of things you wouldn't care about if you were in a car: wind, rain, hills, dogs, even coots. On a lovely May morning, as I pedaled through Zuid-Kennemerland National Park, I cared about coots. I also cared about Edward Abbey. As the bicycle was Abbey's preferred mode in national parks, he surely smiled his approval from beyond the veil.

The Netherlands, we all know, is the land of windmills, wooden shoes, and bicycles. I ignored the windmills and wooden shoes, but the bicycle had proven a revelation. While my family slept in a quaint barn-turned-Airbnb, I settled my sore bum on an uncomfortable seat and pedaled into the national park. A red rump was a small price to pay for the beasts I encountered: placid, long-horned cattle, fallow deer that barked like dogs, shaggy-maned horses, and a few lumbering wisent.

It was the coots that made me skid to a stop.

Up to this point, loons had captivated me, frogmouths had captured my imagination, and goshawks had flown through my dreams. Coots? They were merely drab, charbroiled chickens, the commonplace, aquatic equivalent of the house sparrow. But here, in a two-wheeled land of novelty, the ebony-coated coot, Wite Out spilling down its forehead, stopped me cold. Their appearance was similar to their monochrome American counterparts, but they were chasing each other in vicious frenzies in the shallow ponds. They sparred with the pluck and grit of gladiators, whacking one another with stiff wing beats and karate kicks. Here were some real angry birds.

Battles had long marked this land. The ruins of Brederode Castle flanked the park's eastern side. Well before a colonial foot touched the New World, Brederode was built, besieged and destroyed—twice. Centuries later, during World War II, the Germans used the park for target practice, dropping concrete bombs on "ships" fashioned out of sand dunes. In 1995, against this battleground backdrop, the park was born.

The Dutch were late to the idea of a national park. With a nod to some thirteenth century communally held lands in Mongolia, the US gets the lion's share of the credit for parks with Yellowstone's birth in 1872. But like much America's history, Yellowstone's acquisition and gazettement has a checkered past, fraught with manipulation, persecution, and eviction of native peoples. Though the means were dodgy, the ends—public lands in the form of national forests and parks—are a remarkable idea, affirmed again and again by the many countries that have followed suit and created their own.

Public lands are common. They're also a common, too much a truism to notice, or care about—like coots. Had I not studied environmental science at the University of California at Santa Barbara, I wouldn't have cared either. But there, as I pedaled to class along the western edge of the North American continent, one of the Earth's mightiest commons refreshed me daily: the Pacific Ocean. Perhaps it wasn't surprising that just a few decades earlier at the same university, an economist named Garrett Hardin, seized upon such a—cough, cough—uncommon idea.

Ten years before he retired in 1978, Hardin published "The Tragedy of the Commons," which quickly cemented itself into our national mindset. It's a memorable expression and a highly applicable concept:

You need only walk into a public restroom to validate its truth. (Thankfully, Hardin used cows to illustrate his thesis, not restrooms.) In just six pages, he examined the grazing lands of medieval and post-medieval England: When land is public, he argued, it behooves every cattle owner to maximize their own return—increasing their milk and beef production—by adding one more cow. As every owner does this, the pasture shrinks. It becomes overgrazed. Each owner suffers. Each cow suffers. Udder tragedy.

Had Hardin limited his findings to bovine, the only tragedy would have been an ignored paper with minimal citations; he didn't. Hardin generalized, musing on communally held resources everywhere. Many resources, like oil and fish stocks are finite; their overuse, begat by overconsumption, threaten people everywhere. But since people are rational, he argued, any resource that is communal and unregulated will incentivize each person to take as much as they can. And he's right: At my university's unguarded, food-laden event tables, my small, plastic saucer runneth over. When nobody's looking, my pockets runneth over too.

Economists and environmentalists stampeded over to Hardin's thesis, though recent critics have tempered his ideas. He has been accused of oversimplification, and his role as a director of the American Eugenics Society certainly hasn't helped. Some have gone further. In *Environmental Ethics,* Susan Cox declared that his understanding of the medieval and postmedieval commons was flat-out wrong, writing that "the English common was not available to the general public but only to certain individuals who inherited or were granted the right to use it."

If the commons isn't a tragedy, what is it? Cox claims it's simply a memorialization of fiction—mere Tonypandy. Elinor Ostrom, a Nobel Prize winner I've long admired, suggests instead that it's a drama because the outcome isn't always known: If a community develops institutions or rules of use, its commons can be managed well and tragedy perhaps avoided. Ostrom's undoubtedly right, but drama of the commons just isn't, well, dramatic enough.

Though Hardin and I shared a university and I've used his catchy phrase, I do side with Ostrom. Be warned, though: My belief that tragedies of the commons can be avoided stems from a bad case of cooties I caught from a particularly generous rocket scientist.

We met in a cute little town of canals, cathedrals, and coots, in Delft. Near the end of my family's trip to the Netherlands, we opted for Delft over a visit to louder, more lurid Amsterdam. On the train ride over, a graduate student—Quincy Booster—overheard our debate about what to see in town. "How about I show you around?" he offered amiably. "I've been studying aeronautical engineering here for a few years."

"Aeronautical engineering?" I asked.

"Yeah, I'm planning to be a rocket scientist." Linda and I looked at each other and shrugged. Why not?

"You have time?"

"The whole afternoon," Quincy said, smiling. An hour later, Quincy out in front, we kept our familial squabbling in check and strolled down the postcard-worthy, cobbled streets. He had much to show us: Centuries old stone gates, the painter Vermeer's house, and the leaning tower of Oude Kerk. (I still wonder why Pisa gets all the credit.) While the kids angled for trinket shops and Quincy explained Dutch history to Linda, I lagged behind. There, in one of Delft's stagnant, narrow canals, I contacted cooties.

Cootlets. Cootlings. Baby EUCOs. Whatever you call them, cuties they weren't. Haggard mini-vultures, maybe, as if they had been smashed over the head with ketchup bottles. They were everywhere: Dodging canal boats, slapping across streets, and some—this was the Netherlands—engaged in Red Light District antics all their own. Coot parents and their scraggily little cootsicles paddled about the fetid water, their abundance clearly not correlated with good looks.

A confession: I like to appear well-adjusted. On family trips I wear sunglasses to hide my bird scanning. Unless a rarity flies over, my binoculars remain holstered. But in Delft, on that lovely Dutch afternoon,

I lost my decorum. I leaned over railings, lingered on bridges, took photos, and crammed my journal full of notes. Utter cootishness, all of it.

Even nastier looking than the coots themselves were their nests. Unlike the tidy nests in the national park, these canal nests were dirty piles of rubbish. Too trafficked and polluted for vegetation, the city's refuse was all the resourceful coots had to work with: Candy wrappers, bottle caps, sneaker soles, pizza boxes, kite string, cinch straps, Styrofoam. Everything was fair game. Coots with designs on a family snatched anything and everything to prevent their delicate eggs from rolling into the water. One young coot plucked a cigarette butt from the water, appearing to take a long drag before it was swiped by a greedy sibling. Avarice starts early.

Coots are hardly the first birds to make the best out of human debris. Satin bowerbirds are renowned for accessorizing their nests with glittery junk. And I've spied many a nest of catbirds, robins, and orioles fortified with tinsel, twisty-ties, and faded strands of burlap. But these coot nests were different: They were entirely composed of unnatural materials.

All nests require a foundation, however trashy; the canals, with their sheer vertical walls, didn't allow any. And so the Dutch exonerated themselves: at intentionally spaced intervals, they constructed little rafts for the coots to build upon. Quincy fell back to check on me, worried I'd dropped something into the river. "What kind of ducks are they?" he asked, when I pointed at the delightfully trashy avian comedy.

"Coots," I replied, all-too-happy to educate a rocket scientist. "They're rails, not ducks."

"Do you have these in the States?"

"Not this species," I replied. "And our coots aren't trashy." Quincy was silent. Aeronautical engineers don't laugh easily. A couple with a double-wide stroller walked up, curious to what held me spellbound. The mother looked at us quizzically.

"Coots," Quincy replied before I could say anything. "Not ducks."

His lips curled into a subtle smirk. She shrugged, smiled politely, and walked on. Other passersby squinted into the water as if the birds were invisible; to them, I realized, they were. So were their trashy nests, eye-popping orgies, and slap-happy fights—just as invisible as American coots, the commonplace coots of my own life, had long been to me. To appreciate this highly adaptable and commensal rail, I had needed only a change of context. Awe, my peripatetic life reminds me, is the greatest gift that travel bestows.

Geopolitically squeezed after centuries of conflict, Europeans now have a leg up on how to share limited space and manage public lands. Hardin didn't believe that people have the power to work together, that individuals can jointly limit themselves for the benefit of all. Lacking restraint, he argued, preservation can only occur through privatization or total government control. Steeped in the American ethos of privatization, I am an inheritor of this memorialized fiction. And, in my worst moments when ATV rallies coat me in acrid dust, I even agree. But I've now been to Delft, where I've witnessed miracles at work—and play—in an overwrought common. Little rafts of intentionality lurk amid the waste and wreckage, lending purchase to little lobed feet. In the canals of Delft, hope floats.

Will all of us, like Hardin's medieval cattle herders, insist on taking more than our share? Can we agree to leave a little for the lesser beings? Is private ownership the only ultimate solution? Or, can we collectively treat public land with respectfulness and restraint?

We ended the afternoon with our legs hanging over the edge of the canal. Lambent rays of evening sun accentuated the shadows of pedestrians, reflecting them on the glassy, turbid water. "You have to taste these fries!" Quincy said, passing me a large bucket. Just below the dangling soles of our shoes, a tolerant mother coot sat atop her nest, a pyramid of trash. When Ezra extended her a fry, she readily stepped off her nest to accept. There, amid a faded Lego box, plastic bag, flipflop, and packing peanuts were four perfectly pyriform, gray-brown eggs. Another generation of coots would pop out soon.

"Amazing!" I said, pulling out my camera. Quincy's eyebrows went up.

"You think this is good? Just wait until your next visit when I take you to see our spoonbills!" I studied him. Ten minutes ago, he supposedly hadn't known what a coot was.

I don't know if I'll ever see Quincy's spoonbills, but I do know what the tragedy of the commons really is. It has nothing to do with greed, mismanagement, or how many cows we can squeeze onto a pasture. The tragedy of the commons is our failing to notice—and appreciate—all that is there.

Margin

The edge or border of something

"

Leave a one-inch margin on each side," Mrs. Davis, instructed as I sat at my cold metal desk staring down at a blank sheet of loose-leaf paper in front of me. "Your paper should have a little red line running down the left-hand side. If it doesn't, use your thumb as a ruler and steer clear of the edge." I dutifully obeyed and centrally arranged every subsequent sentence. Margins were to be left alone, their purpose, if any, reserved for the red ink correctives of second grade. I've long since rebelled. As an ecologist, a birder, and a remarkably unsuccessful cartoonist, I've lived in the margins ever since.

Cartoonists seize upon the margins, occupying the hazy line between the everyday and the bizarre. In grad school, as I biked along the Pacific, whacky ideas proved a pleasing antidote to the tragedy of the classroom, to the confined, incommodious places where lectures were as resolute as the tide. I'd pass the time sketching one-box cartoons in my notebooks—in the margins, of course—talking giraffes appearing next to sentence fragments regarding limnology and benthic macroinvertebrates. When I had filled a folder, I pedaled my craft to two newspapers who compassionately agreed to publish them, something to fill space in the bottom corner of the Sports section. Lacking syndication—or payment of any kind—my creative efforts failed to generate even enough revenue for pencil lead. Nor was I buried under fan mail. The highest praise I received came from my mother, who addressed me in a birthday card as "my son the cartoonist." When I left for Africa to study conservation, my cartoon career fizzled out as quickly as it began. For its merciful brevity, perhaps it was remarkable.

Not long after, my life went cuckoo more literally. One lazy Sunday afternoon, having assumed professorial duties in western New York, I went for a walkabout. With my typical lack of direction, I left the road and opted to follow the erratic flight of a swallowtail, a butterfly whose agenda I airily wished to discern. It led me through a woodlot and into the edge of a swampy field, full of grassy puddles and ankle-busting hummocks. A rhythmic, three-noted sound pulsated nearby, as if a kid was blasting away with a toy laser gun. The weird sound was everywhere and nowhere. Curious, I kept walking.

Eye-level, on an arcing twig of red-osier dogwood, was the source: a black-billed cuckoo. Like the American goshawk, the cuckoo had long taunted me from an unchecked perch in my field guide. Now I stood face-to-face with one, on this agenda-free afternoon, close enough to touch it with a broomstick. The bird faced me calmly, its creamy underside set off by an earthy cap and an inky eye enveloped in a crimson orbital ring. A juicy green caterpillar squirmed in its gently curved bill. The cuckoo's stoicism struck me; it didn't hop about, flick its wings, wipe its bill, or fidget. It just sat, as motionless as the branch it was on. Only when I shortened the distance to the length of my arm did the bird flinch. Unnerved, it flew off with strong wing-beats, disappearing into the indigo shadow of a hemlock grove.

I stood slack jawed. Intricacy, right here in the margins of my own backyard.

Sadly, mangroves do not grow in the margins of my backyard. To see this unique ecosystem, you have to visit tropical margins. Perhaps due to their legions of mosquitos and impassable miasma of roots, mangroves are among the most marginalized habitats. People prize beaches, not the mangroves that flank them. Fish think otherwise. The trees' interwoven roots provide an aquatic daycare center, where small fish seek shelter from larger fish.

Though safe from finned predators, the daycare denizens aren't safe from the winged variety. For birds, so many mosquitos and little fish make mangroves a calorie-rich commons, a drama well worth visiting. Herons, egrets, kingfishers, warblers, and a bird you'd be forgiven for thinking was a black-billed cuckoo, the aptly named mangrove cuckoo. The secretive presence of this bird was the reason, during a visit to my parents' home in Fort Myers, I woke Ezra up early and dragged him over to J. N. "Ding" Darling National Wildlife Refuge—part of the largest undeveloped mangrove ecosystem in the US. As far as refuges go, alliterative Ding Darling has one of the catchiest names: named after Jay Norton Darling, who, reminiscent of a banding code, contracted his surname and went by Ding.

Like my parents and so many retirees weary of battling the elements, Darling moved to Florida in his later years. There, he fell in love with Sanibel and fought on behalf of the island's avian residents against construction of a causeway to the mainland. Though he lost the causeway battle, Darling saved a sizeable chunk of the island for the birds: He convinced the state to create a new wildlife refuge, which eventually took his name and was incorporated into the national system. "Ducks can't nest on a picket fence," he quipped.

Darling was full of quips, which hung in the public's mind, as he worked on the national stage. Before his Floridian stint, Franklin D. Roosevelt appointed Darling to be the first chief of the Bureau of Biological Survey, forerunner of the Fish and Wildlife Service. There, he worked with Aldo Leopold and others to expand the National Wildlife Refuge System, acquiring some three million acres of public land for refuges. Practically-minded, Darling also brought together a disjointed band of conservationists via his establishment of the National Wildlife Federation. "Eleven million horses running wild couldn't pull a rubber-tired baby buggy to town unless there was a harness to hook them to the load," he remarked. His creativity wasn't limited to organizing.

An artist, Darling started the federal Duck Stamp conservation revenue program which continues to generate millions of dollars for acquisition and protection of wetland habitats. He was also, I'm compelled to mention, a cartoonist. His politically charged cartoons achieved national syndication and won him two Pulitzer Prizes. Darling's work on the margins had something mine noticeably lacked: success.

But doggonit, I have Darling's zeal. And, as Ezra and I trundled across the Sanibel causeway, my resume proudly lacked "failure to prevent a bridge". (Truthfully, I was grateful for the bridge.) Father and son were going cuckoo. Placing a checkmark next to the black-billed cuckoo in my field guide had thrown a glaring spotlight on the mangrove cuckoo, a local bird so surreptitious that I had long deemed it unfindable. But now, after chancing into the black-billed back home, I was fixated. Somewhere in Sanibel, the mangrove was tooting away. All I had to do was get into its habitat. The two birds were so similar, nearly twins except for an orangish wash on the mangrove's belly and the absence of a red orbital ring. The main difference between the two was their choice in habitat: The black-billed hangs around the margins of eastern deciduous woodlots and thickets, while the mangrove cuckoo skulks around—you guessed it—mangroves.

Cuckoos are the James Dean of the bird world. And they know it.

Long and sleek, they chillax, watching all the uptight, dorkier birds fuss, fret, and foment. Part of this diverse family's coolness derives from two basic body forms: slender and arboreal with short tarsi (the cluster of seven articulating bones in the foot), and heavy and terrestrial with long tarsi, like the emblematic roadrunner. Cuckoo feet are cool too. Unlike the peace sign formed by most bird feet, cuckoo toes are zygodactyl: One of the front toes has migrated backwards to join the longer hallux. An ideal grip for swaggering through bramble, they share this X arrangement with woodpeckers.

And swagger they have, enough to pull off their dirtiest deed: brood parasitism. Brood parasitism—tricking other species to raise your offspring—is clearly cuckoo, though it is also practiced by some ducks, reptiles, and fish. Some 40 percent of the 127 species in the cuckoo family practices some form of it, compared to just 1 percent of all other birds. The most dedicated—obligate brood parasites—do it consistently, but others, like the black-billed cuckoo I chanced upon in New York, only occasionally attempt deception. These casual thieves are known to parasitize eleven species—as well as other black-billed cuckoos.

I can't help but like these mischievous birds. They're far better birdwatchers than me. With a gleam in their eye, they sit and they sit and they sit, watching. When they locate a potential host's nest, they set up a checkpoint. When the host slips out to feed, the cuckoo, suavely of course, darts in and lays an egg, sometimes removing one in the process. None the wiser, the host returns and begins incubating, instinct overriding careful discrimination. To their credit, some hosts have caught on to the fowl play and toss out the cuckoo egg. Others are slower on the draw.

Ornithologists long thought that most birds have an ability to recognize their own eggs, which would allow them to spy and eject a foreign cuckoo egg—until a sly experiment by Bernhard Rensch in the 1920s showed this wasn't necessarily so. Like a cuckoo himself, Rensch patiently watched a nesting garden warbler. As soon as the unsuspecting warbler laid a third egg, he swiped all three and replaced it with a clutch of very different eggs from a lesser whitethroat. The ignorant garden warbler returned, failed to notice that the three eggs in her nest were different, and promptly laid a fourth. She did notice that her own egg was different, however, and she ejected it without hesitation. She went on to incubate only the whitethroat's eggs. Poor unfortunate soul.

—

A mile into the refuge wildlife drive, I pulled off the road. "We'll never see a mangrove cuckoo from the car," I said, unbuckling my seatbelt. "Let's hoof it." Ezra nodded and pocketed his phone. Even in

November, the air was muggy as we stopped to watch a spazzy gnat-catcher ricochet through the mangroves in pursuit of sluggish insects. A red-bellied woodpecker kwirred past, followed by a palm warbler. Sometime later, as our list grew, I heard the sound we had come for: an unmusical string of guttural notes that seemed from the Mesozoic Era. "That's it!" I whispered. We halted in the road. Kissing the back of my thumb, I pished, squeaked, and made every noise possible to make a mangrove cuckoo curious. It worked. Seconds later, a stream-lined bird undulated overhead, trailed by another. Both perched near the top of their namesake trees and stared at us.

A car came up behind us, drew parallel, and stopped. Ugh. The passenger window rolled down to reveal a woman with dark, arrow-straight bangs. "Whatcha lookin' at?"

"Mangroves." But my refusal to lower my binoculars blew my cover. These folks knew the code; nobody studies trees with binocu-lars in a wildlife refuge.

"Harold, pull over!" The car whipped ahead and pulled over. "How long has it been here?" the woman asked, jogging up.

"Not long," I replied, pointing at the bird. Harold, likely of some relation, galumphed over weighed down by an assortment of optics dangling around his neck. An oily-haired teenager with low-hanging pants and large headphones emerged more slowly. "Ooh, I see it," she said. "Two of them!" She extended her arm to orient Harold to the cooperative cuckoo pair. The machine gun clicking from Harold's shutter indicated he had the found the birds too. He paused and flashed a thumbs up.

"There is power in the pursuit of feathered things," J. Drew Lan-ham wrote; but there is also, I've found, abject silliness. Satisfied with his shots, Harold gingerly placed his camera and binoculars on the pavement and turned to face his wife. They shared a high five and then did the grandest thing I've ever witnessed in a national wildlife refuge: a well-rehearsed, two-person Scottish Reel. "It's our lifer dance!" the woman exclaimed, nearly knocking her son out with the binoculars twirling around her head. The son rolled his eyes so intensely I thought he might pass out. I loved this trio instantly. Ezra failed to contain a derisory smirk, but they were briefly oblivious in their celebratory dance.

We hung out with the cuckoo couple for a while. Curious, other cars pulled over, some in the know, others wondering what a mangrove cuckoo even was. A smartly dressed guy who stepped out of cherry-red Corvette confessed that despite living in Sanibel for years, this was his first cuckoo sighting. Another woman glanced at the bird and then sped off in hopes of retrieving her husband to see the cuckoos. "We're homeschooling," Harold told me as we chatted in the road. "For biology today, we thought this would be a fun fieldtrip."

I opted against asking the laconic teen whether he agreed. Whatever he thought of his schooling, it had to be more fun than measuring out and avoiding the margins in Mrs. Davis's second-grade class. The kid looked like a rebel-in-the-making. With parents who performed a public lifer dance, how could he not be? I hoped that, in his rebellion, he'd appreciate life around the edges as Darling had and as I did now: a place rife with life, with thievery, duplicity, and mega cool birds.

Panarchy

The structure in which natural, human, and human-natural systems are interlinked in continual adaptive cycles of growth, accumulation, restructuring, and renewal.

I have the intensity to be a top birder. What I lack is exactitude. The best birders mop up detail, and they can ring it out whenever, and on whomever, they please. The presence of sub-moustachial stripes, the speed of a trill, the completeness of an eye-ring, the tone of a belly wash, the tint on a wing bar. Nuance, particularity, exactitude.

Exactitude isn't needed for the American robin. So used to the orange-breasted worm puller, we needn't bother with particulars. "The bird that everybody knows," legendary birder Roger Tory Petersen wrote in his first field guide. Petersen appropriated space from the robin for its cousins in the thrush family, the Turdidae. Many are shades of gray, as if they hung out in a cosmic vacuum cleaner bag before colonizing the world. Back when I still yearned to become a top birder, I set to work on the Turdidae and learned to distinguish the boldly spotted wood thrush and the hermit thrush with its perpetually wagging, turnip-colored tail. But if not singing, my exactitude remained shaky with all the other winged, earth-colored turds.

I particularly loathe the gray-cheeked thrush. It is well named: Its cheeks are gray. But so are the cheeks of the other thrushes who also share a uniform gray-brown back and medley of semi-convergent spots on the breast. Top birders have little trouble separating the gray-cheeked from the other thrushes. With one exception: Bicknell's thrush. The Cornell Lab, widely consulted as the canon of classification, matter-of-factly declares: "Bicknell's thrushes look very similar to gray-cheeked thrushes and often cannot be separated in the field based on field marks." Ha. A bird to foil exactitude. Take that, top birders!

But not too similar to foil the late Canadian ornithologist Henri Ouellet. Most exacting of the lot, he saw the differences between Bicknell's and gray-cheeked so starkly that he made it his first among seven reasons for separating the two species, historically considered one. Convinced, Ouellet petitioned the American Ornithologists Union to eliminate its subspecies status under the gray-cheeked thrush (*Catharus minimus*) and grant Bicknell's full species status. Here's Ouellet's list, from the 1993 edition of the Wilson Bulletin, concerning the Bicknell's thrush he'd hung out with in Quebec:

Has well-marked morphological differences when compared to adjacent populations of gray-cheeked thrush, particularly in size and coloration.

Its breeding and wintering ranges do not overlap with the other ranges of other populations of *C. minimus.*

It has a different song from that of *C. minimus.*

Doesn't respond to playback of *C. minimus.*

It uses different habitats, particularly mixed second-growth stands in coastal and higher parts of *S. Quebec.*

No hybridization.

High level of sequence divergence in the number of fixed fragment patterns as revealed by biochemical analyses.

If you are an exacting, list-loving top birder, you're welcome. If you're less tortured and just skimmed that, simply realize that Ouellet swam in the deep end. Like the bird he petitioned for, he sang a different song than the rest of us. He was careful, thorough, and, as revealed by the eventual decision of the American Ornithologists Union, persuasive. "It is recommended that the bicknelli population be treated as a full species," he concluded. The Union agreed. Two years after Ouellet's petition, they elevated its status from a subspecies of gray-cheeked, *C. minimus*, to its very own: Bicknell's thrush, *C. bicknelli.* Reckless listers like me licked our lips with the announcement. Ouellet's exactitude had given us a new bird to check off our arbitrary lists. But finding and identifying *C. bicknelli* didn't just require exactitude, it required intensity. And good timing.

To shepherd my intensity, I did some research. As Ouellet had noticed, Bicknell's thrush preferred different habitats than the gray-cheeked. In Ouellet's Quebec, the bird preferred mixed second-growth stands in coastal and higher parts of southern Quebec. South of the Canadian border, Bicknell's was just as finicky. But oddly, in northern New England, it had no interest in the coast. Like a hippie at Woodstock, it liked to be high—above three thousand feet—in stunted spruce-fir forest. If the Lilliputian forests had been burnt by fire or damaged by rime ice accumulation the previous winter, all the better. Thick, impenetrable regrowth better concealed their nests.

Finding the bird meant planning accordingly. Serendipitously, I needn't travel to Maine or Quebec. In the northeast portion of the state, New York had a population of Bicknell's thrushes all its own, what Ouellet described as "a relict taxon from a past refugium." A hardy population nested atop a few mountains in the vast Adirondack Park, a six-million-acre mosaic of public and private lands governed by a unique array of easements, restrictions, and rights-of-way. No tragedy for this common, the Park boasted climbing, hiking, skiing, boating, fishing, and back in 1932 and 1980, even the Olympic Games.

The eastern half of the Adirondacks is pustulated by boulder-strewn mountains that rise like a loaf of bread thanks to a subterranean fist of the Earth's mantle punching ever upward. The Adirondacks may be growing taller but they're a far cry from the craggy, castellated Rockies. The Adirondack peaks are smoother and rounder, better resembling the rounded humps of a Bactrian camel. But woe to the hiker who underestimates them. Many feature windy, bald summits subject to fickle conditions. When they were originally surveyed, forty-six Adirondack peaks measured over four thousand feet high. Intrepid hikers conquered the peaks and dubbed themselves—uncreatively—the Forty Sixers. Alas, subsequent measurements by more exacting folks—Ouellet must have been proud—deemed several peaks a squidge below four thousand. But, as every high schooler knows, labels are hard to shed. Any hiker who summits them all, even the few under four thousand, becomes a Forty-Sixer.

Heading toward forty-six years, the number of high peaks seized me with sudden urgency. My number of laps around the sun is likely half over. This is the stretch run. If there is any arbitrary goal I wished to accomplish before my body gave out, the time is now. I'd never find every bird. I needed a quest that offered a degree of finality and help me ease into old age without regret. Why not tackle the Adirondack high peaks? I would make it manageable: A handful each year, a quest to shift my focus, keep me in shape, and deepen my connections. Birds would be up there too. To cement my quest, I named it: Forty-six by Forty-seven. This gave me five years to finish—and find Bicknell's thrush.

Bicknell's thrush is as particular as Ouellet: It doesn't nest on every high peak. Knowing this, I naturally prioritized Bicknellian peaks over non-Bicknellian peaks. A quick perusal of eBird revealed that two—Whiteface Mountain and adjoining Mount Esther—were satisfactorily thrushy. These two, I had to hike alone. Dragging a friend along on an all-day search for a grungy, furtive bird that hung out in tangles of stunted spruce didn't seem wise, especially if I wanted to keep the friend. Besides, when rare bird searching, I preferred solitude. I didn't mind pausing for ten minutes to stare into thickets. I did mind having to justify it to others. Alone, I wouldn't have to worry about anybody else's well-being. Plus, it afforded me time to tap into my most sequestered thoughts, turn them over, and let them wander alongside. White-face, Esther, a picky thrush, and unabashed introversion—a lovely quartet.

A key variable threatened my sound planning: weather. At dawn, I set off from the Wilmington Trailhead in a steady drizzle. Bird focused, I had forgotten to check the forecast. But hey, lightning at the summit was what I needed to be concerned about, not rain. And besides, maybe it would taper off.

It didn't. Thoroughly drenched, I hunkered down two hours later under the spreading arms of a massive oak, the tree's million-odd leaves a makeshift umbrella. I wolfed down handfuls of trail mix and leaned back against the gnarled trunk. How many people had the tree sheltered over the centuries it stood here, I wondered, running a hand over the corrugated bark. Fortified, I wriggled into my soggy pack and continued upslope. I walked for two more hours.

Had I not recognized a stone tower I had seen in postcards of the oft-photographed peak, I wouldn't have known I had reached the summit. But I may as well have been in a mirrorless fitting room, all was white. Whiteface had lived up to its name. I looked at my watch: 11:34 a.m. Other than a sad-looking robin and a few hardy chicka-dees, I hadn't seen—or heard—any birds. Two guys in cheap, wind-whipped ponchos were huddling on the lee side of the tower. From five feet away, I cupped my hands and yelled to them: "Enjoying the sunshine?"

"We're working on our tan," one hollered back, trying to keep his poncho from ripping off.

"Have fun," the other said. "We're out of this hell hole!" They cinched their hoods tighter and scampered down the trail I'd just come up. Not the exacting sort, I thought, walking out on the exposed face. Nothing about this peak was hell-like or hole-like. It was a freezing promontory, one of highest summits in the northeast. And the moment was *not* torturous. It was rapturous.

Endorphins from the hard climb washed over me with the pound-ing rain. My arms rose skyward. Pelted and unable to see, I leaned into the furious wind, exulting in the way it tore at my raincoat and pant-legs. Streams ran down my face. When a gust threatened to knock me backwards, I fell to my knees and palmed the rough, billion-year-old granite. Rock that had once been soft and gooey. Over inconceivable eons, the rock crystallized. Determined to reach daylight, it broke free of the crust and rose. Despite ceaseless pounding, it rises still. A saying of my beloved ecology professor came to mind.

"Take nothing for granite!" I yelled maniacally into the mono-chrome void.

Rocks, of course, form a cycle. Water, and all the elements, follow suit—as do fields, forests, populations, economies, climates, most everything. These cycles affect each other in dynamic interplay. Up close, with so many variables and cycles nested one within one the other, like Matryoshka dolls, results can seem chaotic. Cause and effect, for a research-driven ecologist, is maddeningly difficult to dis-cern. Zoom out, spatially and temporally, and patterns begin to appear.

Lightning strikes a tree, ignites the forest, and reduces fifty acres to nitrogen-rich ash. Aspen seeds blow into the clearing. Blue jays cache—and then forget—acorns. A bear lumbers through, defecates, and spreads blueberry seeds replete with fertilizer. Aspens shoot up through a tangle of blueberry sprouts. Oaks bide their time and ease past the aspens. One hundred years later, the clearing looks like a for-est again, the aspen stand reduced to a barely discernible mat of fungi and shade-tolerant ferns. Two miles away, during a prolonged drought, lightning ignites another tree and the cycle plays on.

Behold the power of panarchy, I remind my students; I am myself repeating the past. With a profound love of the big picture, my doctoral advisor never missed an opportunity to remind me of panarchy; my penchant for neologisms prevented me from forgetting it. Panarchy is a cool word, used among a coterie of human ecologists to describe the interplay between change and persistence. Turn the number eight on its side like an eroded bowtie and add four words around its loops:

growth, accumulation, renewal, and restructuring. All cycles include these four stages. Our tiny lives—a cycle of their own—are wrapped within larger cycles, most beyond our ken. "You can't control these cycles," I tell my students with the zeal of an evangelist, "but you should at least understand them." I want them to understand ecology. But even more, I want them to embrace every moment. They'll blink and be my age. Youth truly is wasted on the young.

I'm wasting my time. A return to dust—renewal—seems impossibly far-fetched in your twenties. In your mid-forties, life's endpoint—also a beginning point—feels plausible, inevitable even. This endpoint, renewal, is a euphemism for collapse, a lightning strike or stock market crash. To avoid the graphic renewal our bodily decay allows other creatures, I stick to trees. Every inch upward an oak grows, the more susceptible it becomes—to windstorms, lightning strikes, and disease. As it ages, the tree hollows out. Insects bore into the wood. Woodpeckers enlarge cavities. Fungal infections set in. The tree weakens, becomes tottery. A storm blows in. Even if no one is around to hear it, the three-hundred-year-old oak hits the ground. Collapse.

It's a cycle. Dead, the giving tree offers shelter, protection, and nutrition to fungi, plants, salamanders, mammals—all interconnected and undergoing dynamic cycles of their own. "In creation," Steven Bouma-Predinger writes, "there is no existence, only coexistence." By the time I've driven this last point home, my somnolent students are also on the verge of collapse.

Everett Ruess understood panarchy. Inveterate wanderer of the American southwest, Ruess descended into Utah's Davis Gulch and never came out. Though his body was never found, his journals were. I lapped up his angsty, intense entries that soar and crash in a cycle all their own. "I have always been unsatisfied with life as most people live it," he wrote. "Always I want to live more intensely and richly." To do so, Ruess wandered the remote backcountry for years, painting and writing, desperately trying to hold onto ephemeral beauty and meaning. "I have seen almost more beauty than I can bear. I am always being overwhelmed. I require it to sustain life."

The cycle of Ruess's life ended prematurely, but he had come to terms. "Finality does not appall me," he wrote in one of his final letters, "and I always seem to enjoy things more intensely because of the certainty that they will not last." And then there's this, Ruess's final stanza from his best poem:

"Here in the utter stillness
High on a lonely cliff-ledge
Where the air is trembling with lightning
I have given the wind my pledge."

Life, of course, doesn't allow for such a sustained elevated state. Ecstatic, arms-to-the-sky moments exist solely because they contrast with the level ground of normal life. At some point we have to come down.

Overwhelmed on Whiteface, the time came to come down. I had forty some peaks to climb over the next five years and today, in this maelstrom, I had a bird to find. Off the tempestuous summit, the wind lessened and the rain finally eased. Back in the stunted spruce-fir forest, the birds shook out their feathers and hesitantly began singing. Enveloped in fog, I took out my journal and started a list. Red-breasted nuthatches, a flock of chickadees, a distant ovenbird. My list lengthened as other songsters found their voices. I crossed a col that connects Whiteface with Mount Esther and began a slow, attentive ascent up uneven terrain. The trail led over a short span of wobbly planks half sunk in a mire. Midway across, a small brown blur whipped across the planks and disappeared. Was it? It had to be. But to count it, I needed exactitude.

I pulled out my camera. Lacking the identification skills of Henri Ouellet, I needed a photo. I sat on a convenient log and squeaked.

Bingo! Curious, the bird popped out of the underbrush and calmly studied me from a balsam bough. Never have I viewed a grungy-headed, smudgy-breasted bird more lovingly. It looked to have just endured a mud fight. Secure in its subalpine, boggy redoubt, the bird was in no rush. It ran its bill through its tail feathers, cocked its head as if posing for a high school photo, and sang—a song I dutifully recorded. Satisfied its Adirondack world was in order, the Bicknell's thrush tucked its wings and dropped back into the foliage, deserting the bough but filling my heart.

I remained on the log for untold minutes. All six million Adirondack acres had condensed into a six-inch, one-ounce ball of brown. Was this bird young? Old? Did it have fledglings? Was it an empty nester? Its small world on this peak was also so big, affected by regional, hemispheric, and even global cycles. How were the cycles of climate, insects, fire, and disease affecting this population of thrushes? (Recent studies didn't look good: Bicknell's thrush had been proclaimed the "Northeast's most vulnerable songbird.") The reasons Bicknell's was vulnerable were predictably ordinary: a fragmented breeding range, a small and shrinking wintering range due to habitat loss, and two straight decades of documented decline. Up here in the utter stillness, the Bicknell's thrush had given the wind its pledge. Would this sighting be my last?

I don't remember any other part of my hike up Whiteface and Esther. My notes—just six words—aren't any help: "No view. Rancid trail. All mud." But I starkly remember the descent: About three-quarters of the way down, at the very place where I took my pack off and ate trail mix, lay the mighty oak. All eighty-odd feet sprawled lengthwise down the trail. Massive limbs lay scattered about like shrapnel. The tree had dragged several smaller trees down along with it.

Collapse. Renewal.

To lend the chilling episode permanence, I took out my journal and made a few exacting notes about the tree and where it fell. Details matter. Thankfully, timing does too.

Epiphenomenon

*A secondary phenomenon
accompanying another and
caused by it.*

WOOD DUCK

Today I slung muck. Just like I did yesterday. And the day before.
I may even do it tomorrow. When muck slinging, my mind becomes a gloriously void, tumbleweed blows across its thoughtless
expanse. Shin deep in the trickle of water I generously call a creek,
I plunge my shovel in the clayey ooze and yank it out. Everything
drips: water off the shovel, sweat off my brow, dopamine from exertion. Such percolation—drip, drip, drip—pulls memories out of the
sequestered ether of my past. Inchoate, thoughts swirl and swim and
shift. Away from the screens and the scrolling, before me is a better
muck—real muck. My shoveling is Sisyphean. But the peace it brings
and cadence it provides—shovel, sling, splash—makes it well worth
the effort. Acoustical clutter dissipates, anxiety slung away with each
shovelful. No knocks on the office door, dinging notifications, or timetable. In the endless cycle of to-do lists, I cherish my lovely to-don't.

It is the spring thaw. As I have during the eleven previous springs,
I tug on my faded muck boots, grab my duct-taped shovel, and bumble down the hill to the shady ravine that faithfully swallowed all the
trash that former generations lazily fed it. Every hard spring rain sends
water shooting through the ravine in a mocha-colored torrent, a Colorado River in miniature. Yielding only to gravity, the urgent mole-

cules carve up the creek like a Thanksgiving turkey. Only the heaviest detritus, long-buried axles and skeletonized bedsprings, remain. Everything else—strips of siding, shoe soles, my troubles—disappear downstream.

An excavator could surpass my futile muck shoveling in minutes. That's not the point. The act of digging is. If pressed, I confess to digging a frog pond, a murky objective at best. Dam building is a curious endeavor for an ecology professor. Rest assured I'm not gunning for hydropower. I confess—I have entertained the idea of a waterwheel, but it isn't in the cards until retirement. I'm not aiming for flood control either. My house sits high and dry from the creek.

Without obstruction, the water that flows through my creek has a mean depth of one inch. Not enough for fish or frogs or the higher vertebrates I love to watch. A little bit of backed up water is all I'm after, an ephemeral habitat to augment the biodiversity already here, akin to what beavers create with their ceaseless tree felling and stick schlepping. I'm realistic. Panfish won't ever ply these waters. The muck is too heavy, my lumbar too vital, and I'd rather play pickleball. The fish I'm after are metaphorical.

At best, for a few weeks or so, my leaky reservoir will coax up periphyton. If the weather is kind, perhaps it will lure water fleas, pond skaters, and long-legged striders to pirouette upon the surface tension. If I'm too sore from shoveling, I'll set a camp chair aside my little ditch and watch. If the sun breaks through, somebody is sure to show up: Dragonflies, frogs, newts, maybe an optimistic turtle. With a food web in place, my dependable pair of phoebes will come. And the thistly grackles will case the place with their sallow, cadaverous eyes. Maybe I'll get a tail-wagging waterthrush or curious kingfisher. Hopeful expectancy is why I shovel.

This place preceded me. I am altering it, creating it, tying myself to it with attentiveness. The recreation of place, I muse. Puddled water. A redoubt for eggs to resist desiccation and larvae to squiggle up to the surface and take flight. Refuge for orgiastic abandon and exponential growth.

Fellow animal, I belong here, my elemental similarity soothing and shocking. Wrung out, my body can fill twenty-two gallons. Water is my mammalian birthplace from whence I came—primordial ooze, a womb. Herein lies my kingdom—Animalia—predicated upon two hydrogen atoms bonded to one oxygen: a simple molecule governing the fate of the world. My body's molecules are bound with these in a ceaseless, nested cycle, a panarchy. Outside my perspiring skin, this orange, iron-laden water will join Hawk Drop Creek, the Genesee River, Lake Ontario, the St. Lawrence Seaway, and finally, the Atlantic. There the molecules will rest—for a time. Then, sun and wind, evaporation and condensation, will bring them back.

My broken reflection stares up at me in the rippled surface. I am part of in the impermanence. I realize it, but realization and reconciliation are different. It's the latter I'm working on. The water that streams off the sides of my shovel teems with more life than I can name; my brief passage here too short to catalog much. I dig to close the distance, for this blessed tableau, to reconcile myself with unbounded time.

My accomplishments amount to a string of blown out dams and a creek that looks like a stretched-out python swallowed three of the seven dwarves. A quaking mire lies in the wake of each failed dam, a discernible record of my ineptitude. Each year, I fib, I'll build a better dam, one that will last. I know better. My resolve too weak, my interests too many, the spring thaw too strong. I shrug and walk back up to the house. All will be washed away soon enough. The digging—serenity—is the point. Life is dizzyingly brief.

There's another—more damning—explanation. My efforts might just be a pitiful manifestation of unresolved control issues. Heaven knows I have them. I accept culpability, but Eve handed me this shovel; damming is in my blood. Ever since my Euro-colonial ancestors laid anchor, we've been busy as a beaver, rerouting, levying, and damming every possible waterway, as if freely flowing water was a cultural affront. "Strive on!" exhorts an inscribed stone on the engineering building at the University of Wyoming. "The control of nature is won, not given." Berms, dikes, ditches, dams—go hand-in-hand with my Protestant past and single-minded edict: domesticate wild nature. Tame the snarling leopard.

Leopards, we all know, can't change their spots. Hurricane Katrina, that breached dikes and levees and ripped apart New Orleans, reminded us of that. Even in those low-lying places where it looks like we've won, like the magical kingdom of Florida governed by a large-eared mouse, subtle risks lurk. John McPhee's *The Control of Nature*, also fit for a footstool, issued an ominous warning. "In making war with nature," he writes, "there was risk of loss in winning."

John Muir, mixed bag that he was, recognized the risk. Hetch Hetchy Valley, with Edenic wildflower meadows on the banks of the sparkling Tuolumne River, he loved most. The valley was part of Yosemite National Park. But a 1906 earthquake triggered a devastating fire in San Francisco. Local officials took action. Unable to control earthquakes, they could reduce the damage they caused. All they needed was a reliable source of water, preferably a vast water storage facility. With an objective to dam the Tuolumne, they applied to the Department of Interior for rights to the river.

Damn it! thought Muir. Angered, he slung some muck himself:

"These temple-destroyers, devotees of ravaging commercialism, seem to have a perfect contempt for nature, and instead of lifting their eyes to the God of the Mountains, lift them to the almighty dollar. Dam Hetch Hetchy! You might as well dam for water tanks the people's cathedrals and churches for no holier temple has ever been consecrated by the heart of man."

Neither Muir's righteous wrath (and run-on sentences) nor national park status was enough to stave off the federal government. San Francisco's population was too big, the political mire too fetid. In 1913, the dam was completed and Muir's holy temple inundated.

The wilderness prophet died the next year which some, including me, attribute to heartbreak over Hetch Hetchy. Muir channeled his intensity toward preservation, a passive management approach. It's a noninterventionist, hands-off approach. To him, the best use of nature was not to use it at all. To others, like Gifford Pinchot, preservationism was akin to benign neglect. In the Allegheny National Forest, with those oozing pumpjacks and boozing quads, I had walked in Pinchot's long shadow as I fruitlessly searched for goshawks. Though I questioned the outworking of the greatest good for the greatest number for the longest time in Allegheny, other national forest experiences hadn't been so bad.

And like it or not, on a human-dominated planet, I've come to realize that Pinchot's active management is here to stay. A hands-on approach to wildlife management has prevented many endangered species, from black-footed ferrets to whooping cranes, from becoming extinct. It's complicated. A thirty-second search on Google Scholar reveals a smattering of multisyllabic terms that pepper the field's technical journals: biodiversity, biocomplexity, deliberate simplification, indefinite rotations, spatial heterogeneity, environmental stability, variable density harvest systems, decadence processes, landscape dysfunction. If you grimaced at that last one, you're in good company. The point is, active management is alive and kicking, an esoteric counterpoint to Muir's simple keep out and keep off.

Muir and Pinchot make easy foils. And thanks to our simplified two-party political system with its baked-in antipathy to nuance, democrats and republicans do, too. Whatever the issue—dams, pipelines, wolves, fossil fuels—middle ground is as hard to find as a bittern in cattails. Values vary widely between the parties, even among those within the same party. Context dependent work requires many approaches—differences in opinion, and disagreements, occur. It's hard to get ducks in a row.

—

How many ducks make a row? One afternoon, knee deep in muck, one duck sufficed. OO-EEK! OO-EEK! OO-EEK! A female wood duck whistled overhead in quickly tightening circles. She had a coffee-colored body and white spectacles framed her frantic eyes. Shallow, staccato wingbeats brought her even with the crowns of the leafless trees. She banked hard, plunged, pulled up, and deftly back-flapped, as if auditioning for *Top Gun*. On a horizontal limb of a hemlock, she came to rest studying her surroundings.

Forget eggs and larvae, invertebrates and frogs. Here was nature's masterpiece! Waddle all these beauties—especially the males—down a catwalk and the wood duck becomes a unanimous finalist. They are avian art palettes: chestnut, green, blue, and red—all the primary colors demarcated by bold lines of black and white, as if a stained-glass window paddled onto a pond.

Far be it for the wood duck to flaunt. Its self-consciousness adds to its iridescent allure. The duck keeps out of the public eye by opting for well-wooded ponds and dun-colored backwaters. Humble waterways of nearly any size suffice. My rumpled ravine with its string of blown out dams was certainly that. Could I play host to such soul-shaking beauty? Had I naively created place for us both? Was there more I could do?

OO-EEK! OO-EEK! OO-EEK! The wood duck shrieked, neck outstretched like a rooster, her urgency palpable. She paused, tilting her head at odd angles. Was she scrutinizing my creek? Scanning for predators? Inspecting for nest holes? Satisfied, she lifted into the air like a helicopter, made a final circle over my yard to gain altitude, and disappeared.

Take off your sandals, the Lord said to Moses, for the place where you are standing is holy ground. Heart pounding, I plunged my shovel blade deep into the muck and let go. Mud-slinging and dam repair would come later. The time had come for hospitality. Unlike many ducks who nest on floating mats of vegetation, wood ducks use tree cavities, often old woodpecker holes. If my visitor was after real estate, so help me I'd offer her some.

Set on luring back my heavenly host, I downloaded easy-to-follow duck house instructions, scooted piles of recyclables to the side, and laid waste to the garage. A day later, after sawing, drilling, pounding, and painting, I affixed the large box with a fist-sized hole to a fifteen-foot pole, wrapped in slippery tin to ward off raccoons with a taste for scrambled eggs. Digging my forte, I excavated a watery hole next to my latest blown-out dam and sunk the top-heavy contraption in. Before I could wrench my muck boots free from the molasses, the artifice slumped forward as the gravity of the situation—ahem—became clear. The box came to rest at a sickly forty-five-degree angle with the ground, the entrance hole hunched over as if about to blow chunks.

With wire, leverage, a half-submerged stepladder, and a popped blood vessel, I wrenched the monstrosity upright and secured it in place. Sweat dripping off my chin, I stepped back and admired my handiwork. Not great. But for a desperate wood duck, it would do.

It would do for an opportunistic family of starlings, too, who soon moved in.

In 1935, Aldo Leopold created a suitable place too. A chicken coup on eighty exhausted acres along the Wisconsin River. Though the trees had been cut and the soil was depleted, opportunities abounded; the floodplain was perfect for hunting, fishing, swimming, birding, writing, research, and restoration—all the things a professor of wildlife management does with a family of six in a place without electricity and plumbing. Dubbed "The Shack," it was a slow-paced antidote to his academic life at the University of Wisconsin-Madison, where the family lived for the rest of the year. Just as soon as they'd shoveled out the chicken poop, the family crammed in.

Leopold was one of the earliest attendees at Yale's school of forestry, started by the first chief of the Forest Service, Gifford Pinchot himself. Upon graduation, Leopold took a position as a ranger in the Apache

National Forest, in New Mexico. Whatever he didn't learn in the class-room, he picked up from Pinchot, his boss. Leopold inventoried land, estimated available timber reserves, documented grazing—all things that active management entailed. The only thing that slowed him down was a bout with Bright's disease, which resulted in kidney failure and a sixteen-month convalescent period. The slowdown leant Leopold meditative perspective, professional distance by which to judge the Pinchot ethos he'd long marinated in.

What he realized, particularly after witnessing the overgrazed landscape in parts of New Mexico's forests, was that in some cases, the best use of a place was minimal use. Not hands-off preservation per se, but a slower, more measured approach. Leopold realized that Pinchot's goals of the greatest good for the greatest number for the longest time, might, in some cases, mean minimizing impact. For Leopold, Muir and Pinchot were complementary, not antagonistic. Management had become too active, too undisciplined. In some public lands, restraint was needed. Sheep, which Muir snidely regarded as hoofed locusts, needed a shepherd. The sheep needed to be removed from public lands. Hey shepherd, flock off! Leopold's prose, thank heavens, was more tasteful than mine:

> Pinchot's promise of development has been made good. The process must, of course, continue indefinitely. But it has already gone far enough to raise the question of whether the policy of development (construed in the narrow sense of industrial development) should continue to govern in abso-lutely every instance, or whether the principle of highest use does not demand that representative portions of some forests be preserved as wilderness.

Leopold pumped the brakes. He reinserted Muir's ideas back into management. The Forest Service listened. Half a million acres of New Mexico's Gila National Forest soon became protected. But with a twist. Thanks to Leopold, the Gila National Forest was designated a wilderness area, a wholly novel idea—and name—for the National Forest System.

On Levee Road, in Baraboo, Wisconsin, I, too, pumped the brakes. I was on a mission to visit Leopold's Shack. Inspired, I had signed up for a two-hour tour. Fresh off my umpteenth reading of Leopold's *Sand County Almanac*, I had committed his well-known land ethic to memory: "A thing is right when it tends to preserve the integrity, stability, and beauty of the biotic community. It is wrong when it tends otherwise." Simple wisdom that inspired my teaching. Now I wanted to see the place that inspired him. I wanted to better understand how a person could find middle ground: embrace Pinchot and Muir simultaneously.

I have pages of notes from that warm afternoon along the Wisconsin River. I sat in Leopold's chair, held his walking stick, and ran my fingers over the worn teeth of his beloved crosscut saw. There in the shack, Leopold's reverent place, his ideas took on flesh. The place had preceded him. But his family worked hard to make it better. "A rare bird or flower need remain no rarer than the people willing to venture their skill in building it a habitat," Leopold wrote. One year after buying the land, the Leopold family planted three thousand native pines. A drought hit. 99 percent of those pines died.

How did the Leopolds respond? By planting more, of course.

Back home, I keep slinging muck. It's late March. Shovel in hand under a slate-gray sky, I head down to the ravine. Before I descend to the creek, I peer down. Ducks. A pair. One brown with white spectacles. The other a kaleidoscope of green and blue and chestnut. Wood ducks! I drop to my knees and crawl to the edge.

The pair paddles atop my reservoir—all three inches of it—rarely straying more than a body length apart. The male, with his intricately painted head, bobs and twirls. The female watches, waits, and mimics him. Around and around they go, bobbing and twirling. My rumpled ravine, full of bedsprings, boot soles, and eleven woebegone dams, is a Shakespearean stage. Two ducks—at long last—in a row. Untold time later, with Leopoldian restraint, I withdraw. The pair may leave. My smile won't.

The pair left. Three days later, the courting ducks disappeared, choosing some other creek and cavity for their family. I am content. For most of us, I think, this is how it goes: brief moments of bedazzling color, unexpected blessings amid mounds of mud and muck. Few of us are graced with Hollywood scripts. Here we are—shin deep—shoveling. Shovel, sling, splash.

How we spend our days, Annie Dillard said, is how we spend our lives. For now, slinging muck feels right. Miracles happen in this water. Mayfly larvae sprout wings and take to the skies. Tadpoles sprout legs, transform, and take to the margins. Newts absorb pharyngeal gills, turn blaze orange, and take to the land. Phoebes swoop. Waterthrushes wag. Kingfishers rattle. And this spring, in a stagnant, murky pool, wood ducks dance. Three days is enough. The female couldn't have nested here anyway. Though the starlings have moved on, a cuter, wiser family has bought up the shack. Up above the muck, in my listing duckless house, another miracle—an epiphenomenon—was about to hatch.

Miracle

A surprising and welcome event that is not explicable by natural or scientific laws and is therefore considered to be the work of a divine agency.

"There are two ways to be rich," my professor-mentor Jon Arensen told my anthropology class as he described one of the East African cultures we were studying. "One is by acquiring much, the other is by desiring little." I sensed the import of his words and wrote them down.

All these years later, throughout my travels and searching for place and belonging, his words stayed with me. I want to be rich by desiring little, I really do.

The trouble is: I collect junk. The free stuff mostly, junk I can fashion into other junk. But I'm not above shelling out a few bucks for something really impractical, like the 1950s barn pulley that now sits unused and coiled in my garage like a rat snake. Nor am I too hoity-toity to yank a plank, or an old office chair, from a dumpster. Stuff on a roadside, or on free tables, lures me like a phone does a teen. My trips to the dump are more like an exchange. This will come in handy, I say, strapping a cast-off wood pallet to the top of my car.

But the moment never comes, the thing—curtain rod, cement block, window frame—never comes in handy. Instead, it gets entombed, migrating from the car to the garage to a shed, any one of four. Since the sheds are full, incoming junk now goes under or behind them. Wood ducks are hardly the only creatures I've created a place for; each shed is a rent-free rodent condominium, where they, too, collect. I turn a blind eye to their hoarding tendencies: I belong to them, a fellow packrat, squirreling and squirreling and squirreling. Would the day to use this mountain of junk ever come?

It did, a week after the wood ducks left. Leopold had exonerated me. I no longer felt guilty messing around in my ravine. Days in the creek weren't a departure from real life—they were real life. It was a real place with glorious creatures. Though my culture devalued what happened on the margins, my ecological training and well-being did not.

Cathartic as shoveling was, perhaps there was another approach to slinging the muck of daily life. What if, I wondered, I left the muck where it was? Rather than risk another boot to the mire, what if I bypassed it instead?

So on a blissful, unscheduled Saturday afternoon, I marched over to my outbuildings and started pulling out junk. Old boards, broken cement blocks, balls of wire, rusty metal poles—everything—came out. My insensitive purge horrified the legion of winged and whiskered tenants. A surly mouse leapt off the back of a two-by-six, gave me the finger, and scampered away. A scowling flying squirrel sailed over my head and disappeared down the ravine. Confident the uprooted army would regroup, I remorselessly forged ahead. The time had come to build a boardwalk.

Inspiration didn't come via Monopoly's prized property. I had long abandoned the game. It's too long, life's too short, and I no longer fancied spending my remaining days focused upon the capitalistic ruination of my opponents. Monopoly was about acquiring much, precisely the opposite of the rich life I sought. But I did fancy one form of investment—the bird kind. My bird investment had brought me to literal boardwalks, the splintery kind that traverse treacly parts of a trail. Many of my favorites—Magee Marsh, Corkscrew Swamp, a half-submerged one in Pictured Rocks National Lakeshore, were nondescript, warped walkways that snaked through the soupiest stretches of these biodiverse areas. Boardwalks lent purchase to inaccessible places, long marginalized habitats rich in wonder and life. Early morning sojourns on boardwalks had granted me eye-level looks at prothonotary warblers, American bitterns, trumpeter swans, and once, at a five-foot-tall, sour cream-colored whooping crane. The transformative power of elevated, side-by-side planks is uncanny. Each step makes you more attentive and expectant, like following a rainbow. Biological surprise is baked into the boards. On a boardwalk in Florida's Paynes Prairie Preserve State Park, unblinking gator eyes followed my awe-stricken progress. In the middle, where a spiky saw palmetto poked up from the soup, I paused and leaned against the railing. Atop a table-sized leaf perched a purple gallinule. The radioactive bird casually extended a cobalt wing and preened. So close I could offer assistance, I squelched the urge and walked on, feeling like Cortes after gazing upon a sparkling Aztec city.

That's as far as I'm comfortable taking any analogy with Hernán Cortés. Motivated by monetary riches, Cortes chased the antithesis of a birder's reward. I was after the free stuff: Connection, meaning, relationship to a place. These were readily available in my three-acre lot. Attainment seemed a two-part invention: intentionality and being, one begetting the other. Materials in place, I set to work.

But boardwalk construction, I discovered, required more than mere intentionality and being—it required skills. I sketched out a chosen route over the morass, dropped down some cement blocks, and promptly ... watched them disappear. That wouldn't do. I dug some more, dredged, piled, and tried again. So much for sparing my back. This time, the blocks remained above the amoeboid ooze. Satisfied I laid pallets atop them and repeated the process, again and again. What began as a quiescent diversion to my day job became obsessive.

"Eli, if you spent just a quarter of the time you spend in the creek cleaning up the basement, we'd finish it in no time."

"Linda, I'm planning on it."

"When?"

"Soon."

"When?"

"I only have one more section to finish."

"You said that last week." She had me there. One more section had presented unforeseen engineering challenges, a hydrological pattern I hadn't anticipated. One spot wouldn't be drained. No worries. Forget cement blocks. I'd use piers. I spied logs, abandoned under a powerline cut, and rolled them down the ravine. Interlocked like a log cabin, the boardwalk's foundation slowly arose above the muck. With just a few more logs and a few more planks, I would walk where no man had walked before.

"Eli, do you go to the creek to get away from me?" Linda asked one day.

"Of course not," I replied sincerely, slipping into my muck boots, which had taken up permanent residence by the back door.

"You go down every single night."

"Not last night," I replied defensively, "we went to Indigo's band concert." Linda rolled her eyes.

"You know what I mean." I did know what she meant. So restorative had my silly project been that I'd become a bona fide boardwalkaholic, lost in unexpected inebriation. The truth was, I hoped Linda would join in.

The kids eventually did. Wrestling with a log, I glanced up to see now seven-year-old Willow, coat unzipped, spade in hand, smiling ear-to-ear. "I'm here to help!" she announced, jumping into the mud. After ten minutes of chatter, she asked a question—the question—I'd been asking myself since the Pandemic and midlife had derailed my train and caused a one-man pileup. "Dad, what are you doing anyway?" I wiped a dollop of mud off my arm, sucked in my teeth, and looked at her.

"I'm trying to connect this place to that one," I said pointing from where I was to where I wanted to go. Willow nodded and then asked the inevitable follow-up.

"Why?"

I thought about introducing Willow to the idea of existential questioning. And explaining how layers of abstraction had left me bereft of purpose and meaning. I settled on an analogy instead. "Do you see all this muck?" I asked, pointing with my shovel.

"Yeah."

"That's like our life." Willow wiggled her boot in the mud, gears turning. I pressed on. "We all have to get through it somehow. We can plow through and get stuck. Or, we can try to rise above..." I never finished.

"Dad, my boot!"

"What about it?"

"It's gone!"

"That's why I'm making a boardwalk," I said with a wink, steadying her as I fished her lost boot out of the mud.

Though her stints were often shortened by unplanned baptisms, Willow became a ravine regular. Indigo came down a week later. Twelve-years-old, she brought another level of sophistication to the enterprise. "Dad, forget the boardwalk. What you really need to build in this first pool is an island. A place where I can come and read."

"You're right," I said. "But how would you reach it?" Indigo thought for a moment.

"A bridge."

"Otherwise known as a boardwalk," I said, winking.

"Funny," she replied, rolling her eyes.

When the golden buds of the hickories started to unfurl, down traipsed fifteen-year-old Ezra. Like Willow, his coat was unzipped and his footwear—blaze-orange crocs—clearly indicated his participation would be shallow, his eye more critical. His first line confirmed my hunch. "These planks aren't secure," he said, testing out my handiwork.

"You're not secure," I remarked defensively.

"Also," he said, ignoring my quip, "the bridge to the island isn't centered."

"Go for it," I said, handing him a shovel. Unexpectedly, he took it and for the next twenty minutes, recentered the bridge.

With the kids on board, ravine renovation moved into high gear. "Willow's Washtub," an ironically named pool that only made her muddier, assumed a collection of bottles, tubes, and tins she toted down from the garage. "Indigo's Island" appeared next, a heap of earth and logs connected via—you guessed it—a boardwalk. The island, under the nose of the listing duck house, was an unexpected engineering success. So much so that Willow began to rue her lowly washtub. "Dad," she proclaimed, "if Indi gets an island, I should get a treehouse!"

Willow's sense of inequity, Indigo's vision, and Ezra's supervisory critiques led to an epiphany about the dumpy ravine itself, the space we shared. Boundaryless and ineffable at first, intentionality and being gradually turned the dingy water into wine. Space became place.

In a sense, I'd witnessed this miracle on every trip I took, every country I visited, and with every bird I followed. As I communed with the creatures and the people who loved them, map dots became meaningful, and memories attached like barnacles. I noticed something, too: My kids changed the way I interacted with the ravine. They enlivened it. But the significance of the place wasn't contingent upon their presence. It wasn't contingent on anybody's, except for my own. It hung on whatever I brought to it—the receptivity of my senses and my heart. Before my children came, and well after they left, I wasn't ever alone. My sense of place depended only on my interaction with it, which deepened every time I set out.

One still evening in late April, as I hammered nails into the last remaining planks, scratchy sounds emanated out of the duck house's entrance hole. Had I not been right underneath the box, I wouldn't have heard it. So squirrels have accessed it, I thought glumly. When I glanced up, eyes looked into mine. Two pairs of wide, straw-colored eyes, set in two flat, fluffy faces. Baby Eastern screech owls.

In his book, *A World on the Wing*, Scott Weidensaul writes about how the word "reclamation" is often used in regard to the improvement of land or developing it somehow. "This suggests," he concludes, "humanity taking something that had been stolen when in fact the opposite is true." I agree. The creek hadn't belonged to the previous owners any more than it did to me. And while the Seneca had used it well before all of us, it hadn't belonged to them either. They had always understood that. It had preceded them and would outlast us all. It was space that all of us—the Seneca, my family, screech owls—transformed into place via relationship. We could do it well with wonder-filled intentionality, poorly with abuse and neglect, or fail to transform it at all. Of course I hadn't reclaimed the creek. With intentionality and being, the creek had reclaimed me.

My boardwalk is so bad that it doesn't merit the term. It isn't long, two school buses at most. The pallets of wood are mismatched, unlevel, and many planks threaten to split apart with a misplaced step. As Linda likes to remind me, the whole apparatus will surely end up far downstream. But for a season at least, it lifted me up and took me where I wanted to go. A place where owls make me rich.

Acknowledgements

While on Santa Cruz Island last year with my students, a Galapágos giant tortoise lumbered by. On the three-hundred pound chelonian's back was a happy-go-lucky hitchhiker—a half-ounce yellow warbler. It's apt imagery: while flitting about the globe, I have been carried along by the oversized generosity of many; none of whom, other than cab driver Nick, asked anything in return (was the fare that high to go three miles down the road?). I'm humbled and grateful. In the words of Marcel Proust, each of the following special souls gave me new eyes on my voyage of discovery.

In quasi-chronological order that these folks—you all—appear in the text, and some who don't, here goes (my gratitude compels me to personalize):

J. L. Miller and whip cracking Silas: I never would have visited a golf dome, nor seen the peregrine, had you not invited me along. Your friendship has proven more consistent than our golf swings.

British twitchers in Royal Harbor: thanks for appreciating big green birds and not calling the cops as I did the same.

Michael and Julia Beardsley—were it not for your hospitality and Flaco fandom, I never would have glimpsed that wise, lonely bird. To my 2023 Field Botany class, thanks for pretending to feign interest in plants as we pursued Flaco. Owl's well that ends well.

Colin, Ingrid, Zoe, and my entire 2021 Human Ecology class: yes, the universe is as complicated as it appears. But my thankfulness for your searching souls isn't.

Au Sable Institute class of 2022: kudos for exposing my hypocrisy. Stay loony. And to my stoical Isle Royale pilot: thanks for keeping that float plane in the sky, and my breakfast in my stomach.

Andrew Knapp: the Grand River is not your yard. You neither tend it nor mow it. Remove those birds and I'll be even more grateful for your growing bird love. Watching you pursue birds has brought me more happiness than your "help" with this book.

Larry Proffitt: you're right, discretion is the better part of valor. Thanks for showing me both and letting me gobble up your wisdom. Grandpa Knapp: thanks for investing in vertiginous real estate, Larry Proffitt, and me.

Ella Sorensen: The Great Salt Lake's birds are lucky to have you. You're the shrewdest burrowing owl I know.

Mom: you are a woman of great faith, limited fantasy wins, and a lightning-fast cord puller. Thanks for liking me more than Joe Biden. Dad: only you can make cardiac arrest recovery that memorable. After sneaking out of the hospital, I'm grateful you snuck back in. Thanks for reminding me that your middle son (and Earth) is not alone. Emergency responders who resurrected Dad: you are too legit to quit.

Rodney Graham: you farm—and live—the right way. Thanks for opening your land—and heart—to me. May mockingbirds and nighthawks forever fly over Fort Hill. To our tour guide at Monticello: you are original.

Mariis "Mossy" Kilcher: the song of the fox sparrow—and your song—mean much. Thanks for demonstrating how to listen.

Debi Shearwater: you live up to your sleek surname. Thanks for delaying retirement long enough for me to board. To the booby lady: you're right—pelagic birds are worth shouting for. Thanks for refraining from the urge to shove me overboard.

Fleur Ng'weno: thanks for your dedication, identification skills, and demonstrating the importance of data. And for dusting off words like "coxswain." And to our dear Coxswain: no amount of water hyacinth can hold you back. I would board any boat, no matter how leaky, with you as my captain. Don Turner: thanks for educating my students and redirecting all their imperialistic guilt toward China. To the Kenyans in my boat: no bird flies past you unseen. I don't egret any time with you.

Barb and Lisa Arensen: while this book is dedicated to Bwana Jon, my life has been enriched by every Arensen I've hiked, camped, birded, kayaked, golfed, and worked with. As far as families go—nuclear and extended—none are better.

John Lyon: thanks for giving me the chance to be serenaded by the soul-shattering sound of northern white-cheeked crested gibbon. Kyle Burrichter: thanks for taking your job seriously, setting that hideous alarm, bossing me around in the jungle, and constructing the world's greatest bird blind. Someday we'll find a real rarity in your pond. Kelly Mohnkern: thanks for reminding me of what's truly important in these ecological endeavors. Salah, Hong, and all my supernatural Cambodian guides: thanks for revealing what a real birder is.

To my 2022 Ornithology class: thanks for enduring the sun, rain, flat tires, cockroaches, and heinous shrieking of the Puerto Rican parrot. To Jose: we will never forget your sincere, indomitable spirit. Seagull Steve: I can only dream of writing a travel blog as particularly memorable as yours.

Aussie cab driver Nick: thanks for making me self-reliant. Earbud guy on that drizzly day in Woodlands Historic Park: thanks for coming down from heaven to rescue me, and letting me retain my limbs. Sri Lankan salon family at Roo Hair and Beauty: you could—and should—have shooed me out. Thanks for being a port in a literal storm. I wish you'd talked me into a makeover. Snoring compatriots at YHC hostel in Melbourne: well, at least I didn't oversleep. Anonymous employee at the Royal Botanic Gardens in Melbourne: thanks for leading me to the Guadeloupe Island oak. Without you, I never would have spied a frogmouth.

Elise: thanks for working with hellbenders and goshawks and motivating me to go the wild things are.

Quincy Booster: you deftly propelled us through Delft. My affection for you isn't rocket science.

Lifer dance Ding Darling couple: you two embody what makes birding fun. Thanks for seeing through my rudeness and not letting a cuckoo teen hold you back.

Whiteface hikers: way to brave the elements. Thanks for reminding me I'm not the only one in this world with questionable judgment. Christy and Heidi Shea: thanks for a weekly WhatsApp barrage of Wissahickon birdsong and fiery sunsets from Fancher Heights. Dad Shea: thanks in advance for your marketing work. Mum Shea: so much familial nature appreciation traces back to you.

Ethan Knapp: for an A-plus tour guide, you're a pathetic birder. But you certainly know your turkeys.

Nathan Peace, thanks for corrections, technicalities, and efficiency. From Matema to Malewa to Mbeya Peak to Mumbai (hopefully), thanks for being a geographically faithful friend. May I be at your side when you see a snowy owl.

KEA members, keep slogging out to the swamps in pursuit of the ultimate grainy, inconclusive photograph in our ridiculous quest of feathered futility. May each of you claim an arbitrary category all your own.

Torrey House family, thanks for welcoming me into the nest and encouraging me to fly. Pun loving Quinn: I've appreciated our correspondence. Lark: I pray our migratory routes continue to converge. Scout: your organizational skills and patience are second-to-none. Gray: thanks for being there when I needed you. Kathleen: if readers judge my book by its cover, I'm in great shape. Kirsten: thank you for recognizing value in my work all those years ago and nurturing my growth as a writer. Your mark on my vocation—my life—is indelible. Will: you are visionary, generous, thoughtful, hilarious, and tireless. Adrift on a choppy sea of my own melodramatic making, you spied land and grabbed the tiller. Thanks for all the phone calls, all the zooms, all the emails, all the missed deadlines, and making an overcast afternoon in Binghamton spring into color. More importantly, thanks for being a friend.

Linda: you are the quintessence—and love—of my life. Thanks for all your encouragement, these beautiful illustrations, and creating place with me. Ezra, Indigo, and Willow: your companionship, sense of adventure, unsolicited critiques, laughter and joy animate my life and make my days much fuller than my hair. Thanks for lending meaning to the muck.

To the Ojibwe, Cherokee, Seneca and all people who came before: thanks for understanding the importance of place and revealing proper relationship. May we all follow your lead.

And to God: thank you for making such a glorious place. Thank you for letting giant tortoises lumber across the ground and half-ounce yellow warblers ride that upon their backs.

About the Author

Eli J. Knapp, PhD, is a professor of Environmental Science at Houghton University, in New York. Interested in experiential learning, he has taken family, friends, and students to countries throughout the world including fifteen times to Africa. Birds have been constant companions in his travels, featuring as the primary subject of his two books, *The Delightful Horror of Family Birding: Sharing Nature with the Next Generation*, and *Dead Serious: Wild Hope Amid the Sixth Extinction*. He lives with his wife, Linda, and three children, Ezra, Indigo, and Willow, in Fillmore, New York.

About the Illustrator

Linda Knapp was born and raised in Sierra Leone, West Africa, where a passion for other cultures led her to acquire a B.A. in Intercultural Studies (from Houghton College) and an M.A. in Cultural Anthropology (from Colorado State University). Through that journey she met and married author, Eli Knapp. Together they conducted fieldwork in Human Ecology in Serengeti National Park, led a college study abroad program in East Africa from 2009 to 2022, and are raising three kids, Ezra, Indigo, and Willow. In addition to being mother and homemaker, Linda's formal employment has included being an adjunct professor of Anthropology, an Art Gallery director, and currently the Houghton University Art Collection Manager.

About the Cover Art

In the realm of contemporary art and photography, few artists navigate the delicate interplay between science and creativity as masterfully as Xavi Bou. A visual artist based in Barcelona, Bou has spent over a decade capturing the unseen beauty of the natural world, revealing its hidden rhythms and movements. His groundbreaking project, Ornitographies, transforms the ephemeral flights of birds into mesmerizing visual symphonies, transcending the limits of traditional wildlife photography.

Through innovative techniques, Bou's work transforms fleeting moments into tangible, organic shapes, ethereal trails that speak of grace, instinct, and the delicate choreography of nature. His images do not simply depict birds in flight; they unveil the invisible, drawing viewers into a world of abstraction where art meets the intricacies of the animal kingdom.

With Ornitographies, Bou invites us to reconsider the way we perceive the natural world. It is an ode to the skies and their winged travelers, a reminder of the beauty we often overlook. His work compels us to pause, look up, and marvel at the patterns of life unfolding above us, a silent testament to the profound interconnectedness of all living beings.

Torrey House Press

Torrey House Press exists at the intersection of the literary arts and environmental advocacy. THP publishes books that elevate diverse perspectives, explore relationships with place, and deepen our connections to the natural world and to each other. THP inspires ideas, conversation, and action on issues that link the American West to the past, present, and future of the ever-changing Earth.

Visit www.torreyhouse.org for reading group discussion guides, author interviews, and more.

As a 501(c)(3) nonprofit publisher, our work is made possible by generous donations from readers like you.

Join the Torrey House Press family and give today at
www.torreyhouse.org/give.

Torrey House Press is supported by Back of Beyond Books, Bright Side Bookshop, The King's English Bookshop, Maria's Bookshop, the Jeffrey S. & Helen H. Cardon Foundation, the Lawrence T. Dee Janet T. Dee Foundation, the Stewart Family Foundation, the Barker Foundation, Robert Aagard & Camille Bailey Aagard, Kif Augustine Adams & Stirling Adams, James Allen, Diana Allison, Richard Baker, Patti Baynham & Owen Baynham, Klaus Bielefeldt, Joe Breddan, Karen Buchi & Kenneth Buchi, Rose Chilcoat & Mark Franklin, Linc Cornell & Lois Cornell, Susan Cushman & Charlie Quimby, Lynn de Freitas & Patrick de Freitas, Pert Eilers, Betsy Gaines Quammen & David Quammen, Laurie Hilyer, Phyllis Hockett, Kirtly Parker Jones, Rick Klass, Jen Lawton & John Thomas, Susan Markley, Leigh Meigs & Stephen Meigs, Kathleen Metcalf, Donaree Neville & Douglas Neville, Laura Paskus, Katie Pearce, Marion S. Robinson, Molly Swonger, Shelby Tisdale, the Utah Division of Arts & Museums, Utah Humanities, the National Endowment for the Humanities, the National Endowment for the Arts, the Salt Lake City Arts Council, and Salt Lake County Zoo, Arts & Parks. Our thanks to individual donors, members, and the Torrey House Press board of directors for their valued support.